# BEYOND ONE SQUARE MILE

A COLLECTION OF RECIPES CELEBRATING 60 YEARS OF THE JUNIOR LEAGUE OF BRONXVILLE

# BEYOND ONE SQUARE MILE

## A COLLECTION OF RECIPES CELEBRATING 60 YEARS OF THE JUNIOR LEAGUE OF BRONXVILLE

Published by The Junior League of Bronxville, Inc.
Copyright © 2009 by The Junior League of Bronxville, Inc.
135 Midland Avenue/P.O. Box 430
Bronxville, New York 10708-0430
914-793-5097

All photographs courtesy of the Village of Bronxville Historian.
Recipe page line art by Rossana Valentino.

This cookbook is a collection of favorite recipes, which are not necessarily original recipes.

ISBN: 978-0-615-21097-1

Edited, Designed, and Produced by

**Community**Classics™

an imprint of

FRP

a wholly owned subsidiary of Southwestern/Great American, Inc.
P. O. Box 305142
Nashville, Tennessee 37230
800-358-0560

Manufactured in the United States of America
First Printing: 2009
4,000 copies

Proceeds from the sale of *Beyond One Square Mile:*
*A Collection of Recipes Celebrating 60 Years of The Junior League of Bronxville* will benefit the community and the charitable works of The Junior League of Bronxville, Inc.

If not stated otherwise all ovens are assumed
to have been preheated.

# TABLE OF CONTENTS

&#x2766;

# Acknowledgments

✂

We would like to acknowledge the tireless efforts of the members of the cookbook committee. We tested, tasted, and analyzed a lot of recipes! This book is proof of their enormous talents and spectacular creativity.

We would also like to thank all the members of The Junior League of Bronxville for sharing their favorite recipes with us. Without all of your contributions, there would not be a cookbook.

Thank you to you all.

Candace Martin & Raquelle Frenchman

## Cookbook committee

✂

Raquelle Frenchman, Co-Chair
Candace Martin, Co-Chair
Anne Erblich
Suzanne Klein
Andre Koester
Joanne Leopold
Susie Reisinger
Jen Ungvary
Rossana Valentino
Donia Vance
Heidi von Maur

# INTRODUCTION

This book celebrates all of the small pieces that create the whole of The Junior League of Bronxville. The Junior League of Bronxville has a diverse membership, a wide-reaching geographical range, and cutting-edge programs in each of the five service areas that our League assists.

Geographically, the Village of Bronxville is quite small, just shy of one square mile. However, The Junior League of Bronxville reaches out far beyond these geographical borders and draws members and support from, and provides services to the City of Mount Vernon, the City of Yonkers, the Town of Eastchester, the Village of Tuckahoe, and, of course, the Village of Bronxville. Quite a feat for such a "small" League!

Between the pages of this book you will find a bit of history about our service areas, as well as the programs and services we provide in these areas. Most of all, you will own some fabulous recipes, with personal anecdotes shared by the dedicated women who are striving to improve other people's lives *Beyond One Square Mile*.

5

# PONDFIELD PRELUDES

# The Junior League of Bronxville

*"Pondfield Preludes"*

*The main thoroughfare in the Village of Bronxville, Pondfield Road stretches from
the border of Bronxville and Mount Vernon, all the way into Yonkers, where it becomes
Pondfield Road West in Cedar Knolls.*

The Junior League of Bronxville is an organization of women committed to promoting
voluntarism, developing the potential of women, and to improving the community through
effective action and leadership of trained volunteers. Its purpose is exclusively educational and
charitable. The Junior League of Bronxville serves the communities of Bronxville, Eastchester,
Tuckahoe, Yonkers, and Mount Vernon in Southern Westchester County, New York.

Beginning in 1924, a group of Junior League members who had moved from other
communities to Bronxville began meeting regularly at each other's homes to sew layettes.
In 1948 they joined the Association of Junior Leagues International and became incorporated
as "The Junior League of Bronxville." Since that time, the women of The Junior League
of Bronxville have been volunteering their time and talents to improve the lives of women,
children, families, and the elderly through advocacy work, public policy, program
development, direct care, community-wide events, fund-raising, a discretionary grant
program, scholarships, and awards.

Throughout its history, The Junior League of Bronxville has endeavored to create and
support cutting-edge programs and services in our communities. Here is just a sampling
of our good works throughout our sixty years of service.

*The Stork Exchange, Pennywise and Pennypincher consignment shops*
*Greyston Family Inn and Music and Movement Programs*
*Lawrence Hospital Mobile Library Cart, Gift Shop, and Information Desk*
*Children's Literacy through World Cultures*
*RECYCLE! A community-wide recycling program*
*The Tree House for the Bereavement Center of Westchester*
*Operation Safe Smiles—child identification program*
*Women's Cancer Support*
*Eastchester Community Action Project*
*Done-In-A-Day/Done-In-A-Night*
*Meals on Wheels Ageless Friends*
*Mount Vernon Head Start Bookmaking*
*Wartburg Adult Care*

PHOTO: WINE AND SPIRIT SHOP ON PONDFIELD ROAD

# APPETIZERS AND BEVERAGES

MARINATED OLIVES

AMERICAN DEVILED EGGS

FIGS FILLED WITH GOAT CHEESE AND PROSCIUTTO

BABY RED POTATOES WITH SOUR CREAM AND CAVIAR

SMOKED SALMON TARTARE SLICES

HOT ARTICHOKE DIP

ENDIVE WITH CHUNKY BLUE CHEESE DIP

LIGHT CARAMELIZED ONION DIP

HUMMUS

SMOKED TROUT MOUSSE

TIROPITAS

SLIDERS

MARYLAND CRAB CAKES WITH RÉMOULADE DIP

⁊⁊⁊

OPEN HOUSE PUNCH

CHAMPAGNE RASPBERRY PUNCH

RUBY RED GRAPEFRUIT SPARKLER

LIMEY APRICOT RUM SLUSHY

POMEGRANATE MOJITOS

FRESH MARGARITAS

SPICY BLOODY MARYS

SOUTHSIDERS

WHITE SANGRIA

LONG ISLAND GREEN TEA

# MARINATED OLIVES

*1½ cups brine-cured large green olives with pits*
*1½ cups brine-cured large black olives with pits*
*3 shallots, cut into halves and thinly sliced*
*3 garlic cloves, crushed*
*2 tablespoons Pernod*
*1 teaspoon grated orange zest*
*1 teaspoon red pepper flakes*
*¾ teaspoon salt*
*½ teaspoon minced fresh thyme*
*Pinch of cayenne pepper*
*¼ cup extra-virgin olive oil*

Rinse and drain the olives. Pat dry with paper towels. Mix the olives with the shallots, garlic, liqueur, orange zest, red pepper flakes, salt, thyme and cayenne pepper in a bowl. Add the olive oil and toss to coat.

Cover and chill for 12 hours or up to 1 week. Bring the olives to room temperature before serving.

*Makes 3 cups*

*THESE OLIVES ARE PERFECT TO HAVE ON HAND WHEN GUESTS DROP BY. WHEN YOU TELL THEM YOU CREATED THE MARINADE YOURSELF, ACCEPT THE COMPLIMENTS—BUT DON'T LET ON HOW EASY IT REALLY WAS! DON'T FORGET TO PUT OUT A SMALL BOWL FOR THE OLIVE PITS!*

# AMERICAN DEVILED EGGS

*6 eggs*
*1 tablespoon minced fresh chives*
*1 teaspoon Dijon mustard*
*¼ teaspoon freshly ground pepper*
*1 or 2 dashes of Tabasco sauce*
*Salt to taste*
*3 tablespoons mayonnaise*
*Chopped fresh chives to taste*

Place the eggs in a saucepan and rinse gently with warm water. Cover the eggs with cold water and bring to a boil over medium-high heat. Reduce the heat to a gentle simmer and cook for 13 minutes. Drain the eggs and rinse with cold water. Peel the eggs and arrange on a plate. Chill, loosely covered, for 15 minutes.

Slice the eggs lengthwise into halves. Scoop the yolks carefully into a bowl and mash with a fork. Add 1 tablespoon minced chives, the Dijon mustard, pepper, Tabasco sauce and salt and mix well. Stir in the mayonnaise. Mound the egg yolk mixture evenly in the egg white halves.

Arrange the deviled eggs on an egg platter and sprinkle with chopped chives. Garnish with whole chives. The chopped chives and whole chives also make a nice bed for the eggs if you do not have an egg platter.

*Serves 6*

*I HAVE HAD THIS RECIPE SINCE I FIRST STARTED COOKING THIRTY YEARS AGO. IT IS A TRADITIONAL DEVILED EGG RECIPE WITH A KICK. IT IS INCLUDED IN MY UPCOMING HORS D'OEUVRE BOOK TO BE RELEASED SOON.*

# FIGS FILLED WITH GOAT CHEESE AND PROSCIUTTO

*8 figs*
*4 thin slices prosciutto di Parma*
*1 (8-ounce) log chèvre (goat cheese)*
*1 tablespoon chopped fresh rosemary*
*Good-quality olive oil for drizzling*
*Freshly ground pepper to taste*

Cut the figs lengthwise into halves and arrange cut side up on a baking sheet. Cut each prosciutto slice into four pieces. Cut the chèvre into sixteen equal slices.

Layer each fig half with one slice of the chèvre, a light sprinkling of the rosemary and one piece of the prosciutto. Drizzle lightly with olive oil and sprinkle with pepper.

Broil for 3 to 5 minutes or until the prosciutto crisps slightly and the figs are heated through. Serve warm.

*Serves 6 to 8*

*A WONDERFUL AND INTENSELY FLAVORFUL APPETIZER THAT IS PERFECTLY BALANCED IN TEXTURE AND TASTE.*
*A FINE WAY TO USE ALL THE EXTRA FIGS FROM THE VERY PROLIFIC TREES IN MY PARENTS' GARDEN.*

# Baby Red Potatoes with Sour Cream and Caviar

*12 small red potatoes*
*1 cup sour cream*
*1 (2- to 4-ounce) jar caviar*

Arrange the potatoes in a single layer on a baking sheet. Roast at 350 degrees for about 30 minutes or until tender when pierced with a knife, turning occasionally. Let cool slightly and then cut the potatoes into halves.

Arrange the potatoes cut side down on a serving platter. Scoop out some of the top with a melon baller, creating a small cavity.

Fill each potato shell with a dollop of the sour cream and top with some of the caviar. Red caviar is from salmon, black caviar is from sevruga or osetra and golden caviar is from whitefish.

*Makes 4 (3-potato) servings*

*Caviar is always an elegant and festive party food. My husband is not a big fish fan, so I top some of the potatoes with chopped fresh chives and crumbled bacon for him, and everyone is happy.*

# Smoked Salmon Tartare Slices

12 red potatoes, 1½ inches in diameter
1 tablespoon olive oil
Kosher salt to taste
8 ounces smoked salmon, finely chopped
¼ cup finely chopped red onion
2 tablespoons finely chopped fresh chives
Pepper to taste
1½ tablespoons lemon juice
⅓ cup sour cream
1 tablespoon finely chopped fresh chives

Cut the potatoes into ¼-inch-thick slices and toss with the olive oil and salt in a bowl. Arrange in a single layer on a baking sheet and roast at 350 degrees for 30 minutes. Do not disturb the potatoes during the roasting process. Remove to a wire rack to cool.

Combine the salmon, onion, 2 tablespoons chives, salt and pepper in a bowl and mix well. Drain the tartare if needed to discard any excess liquid.

Brush the cooled potato slices with the lemon juice and season with salt and pepper. Top each with a heaping ½ teaspoon of the tartare and a dollop of the sour cream. Sprinkle evenly with 1 tablespoon chives. Arrange on a serving platter and serve immediately.

*Makes 4 dozen*

*This is a really easy hors d'oeuvre, and if you are pressed for time, just serve the tartare on a tasty cracker. But if you have time, make the roasted potato slices to serve the tartare on— your guests will be so impressed.*

# HOT ARTICHOKE DIP

2 (14-ounce) cans artichoke hearts, drained
1 cup mayonnaise
1 cup (4 ounces) grated Parmesan cheese
2 tablespoons grated onion
1/4 teaspoon Worcestershire sauce
1/4 teaspoon lemon juice
Freshly ground pepper to taste
Grated Parmesan cheese to taste

Press the artichokes to remove any remaining moisture and then chop coarsely. Combine the artichokes, mayonnaise, 1 cup cheese, the onion, Worcestershire sauce, lemon juice and pepper in a bowl and mix well. Spread in a baking dish or soufflé dish and sprinkle with remaining cheese to taste.

Bake at 400 degrees for 20 minutes or just until the top is brown and the dip is heated through. Do not overcook as the mayonnaise will liquefy. Serve with assorted party crackers and/or toasted pita triangles.

*Serves 10*

*THIS IS SOMETHING THAT EVERYONE SEEMS TO DEVOUR AT PARTIES, AND AFTER MANY YEARS OF TWEAKING, I THINK THAT I FINALLY FOUND THE PERFECT BALANCE OF INGREDIENTS. DON'T FORGET THE ONION, AS I THINK IT IS THE KEY!*

# ENDIVE WITH CHUNKY BLUE CHEESE DIP

*1 cup sour cream*
*1 cup mayonnaise*
*2 teaspoons freshly ground pepper*
*2 teaspoons Worcestershire sauce*
*¼ teaspoon celery salt*
*2 dashes of Tabasco sauce*
*Sea salt to taste*
*1¾ cups crumbled Gorgonzola cheese*
*1 tablespoon chopped fresh chives*
*4 heads endive, separated into spears*

Combine the sour cream, mayonnaise, pepper, Worcestershire sauce, celery salt, Tabasco sauce and salt in a food processor. Process until blended. Spoon into a bowl and fold in the cheese. Chill, covered, for up to two days.

Stir the chives into the dip. Spoon a generous amount of the dip onto the stem end of each endive spear and arrange on a serving platter.

*Serves 12*

*MY MOM TOSSED THIS TOGETHER MINUTES BEFORE A COCKTAIL PARTY ABOUT FIFTEEN YEARS AGO, AND I HAVE BEEN SERVING IT EVER SINCE—WITH A COUPLE OF TINY ADDITIONS.*

# LIGHT CARAMELIZED ONION DIP

*¼ cup (½ stick) unsalted butter*
*4 Vidalia onions, quartered and sliced*
*1 teaspoon sugar (optional)*
*½ cup sour cream*
*½ cup plain nonfat yogurt*
*4 ounces whipped cream cheese*
*½ teaspoon cayenne pepper*
*Kosher salt and black pepper to taste*

Melt the butter in a large sauté pan over medium heat. Add the onions and sprinkle with the sugar. Cook for 20 to 30 minutes or until the onions are soft and golden brown, stirring occasionally. Let stand until cool.

Combine the sour cream, yogurt, cream cheese and cayenne pepper in a mixing bowl. Beat with an electric mixer fitted with a paddle attachment until combined. Fold in the onions and season with salt and black pepper. Chill, covered, for 1 hour or longer. Taste and adjust the seasonings just before serving.

This may be prepared up to 1 day in advance and refrigerated until serving time. Bring to room temperature before serving. Serve with your favorite potato chips.

*Serves 12*

*I MADE THIS FOR THE GIRLS AT BUNCO, AND THEY LOVED IT!*

# Hummus

*1 (15-ounce) can chick-peas, drained and rinsed*
*¼ cup tahini*
*¼ cup extra-virgin olive oil*
*¼ cup water*
*1 tablespoon fresh lemon juice*
*1 garlic clove, minced or crushed*
*¾ teaspoon salt*
*Cayenne pepper to taste*

Combine the chick-peas, tahini, olive oil, water, lemon juice, garlic, salt and cayenne pepper in a food processor. Process for about 40 seconds or until smooth, scraping the side of the bowl as needed.

Spoon the hummus into a bowl and cover with plastic wrap. Chill for 30 minutes or longer to allow the flavors to blend. Serve chilled with pita chips, fresh pita wedges and/or crudités.

*Serves 6 to 8*

*This dip can be served with pita chips, fresh pita cut into wedges, or with crudités.*
*This homemade recipe beats the one at the supermarket anytime.*

# SMOKED TROUT MOUSSE

*8 ounces smoked trout*
*¼ cup heavy cream*
*Juice of ½ lemon*
*2 tablespoons grated horseradish*
*Salt and pepper to taste*
*8 ounces cream cheese, softened*
*2 to 3 tablespoons heavy cream*

Remove the skin from the trout and discard. Combine the trout, ¼ cup cream, the lemon juice, horseradish, salt and pepper in a food processor. Pulse until combined. Remove to a bowl.

Process the cream cheese and cream in the food processor until light and fluffy. Fold into the trout mixture. Chill, covered, in the refrigerator. Serve with water crackers and/or toasted baguette slices.

*Serves 6*

*WHEN BUYING PACKAGED SMOKED TROUT, LOOK FOR ONE WITH LEMON PEPPER OR GARLIC PEPPER SEASONING AS THAT MAKES IT BOTH TASTIER AND MORE VISUALLY APPEALING. THIS RECIPE ALSO WORKS WELL WITH SMOKED SALMON. I WAS IN MY NEIGHBOR'S KITCHEN WHEN SHE REMEMBERED THAT SHE HAD PROMISED TO BRING AN HORS D'OEUVRE TO A PARTY THAT EVENING. SHE STARTED PULLING THINGS FROM HER REFRIGERATOR AND CABINETS. I ASKED HER WHAT RECIPE SHE HAD USED, AND SHE SAID "RECIPE, WHAT RECIPE? I JUST MADE IT UP." IT IS NOW MY GO-TO RECIPE FOR COCKTAIL PARTIES.*

# TIROPITAS

*1 (16-ounce) package frozen phyllo dough*
*1 pound French feta cheese, crumbled*
*8 ounces small curd cottage cheese*
*8 ounces cream cheese, softened*
*3 egg yolks, lightly beaten*
*1 cup (2 sticks) unsalted butter, melted*

Thaw the phyllo dough using the package directions. Combine the feta cheese, cottage cheese, cream cheese and egg yolks in a bowl and mix well. Unroll the phyllo dough and arrange on a sheet of baking parchment. Cover with another sheet of baking parchment and lay a damp kitchen towel over the top to prevent the pastry sheets from cracking while assembling.

Working with one sheet of the phyllo at a time, cut the sheet lengthwise into 3-inch strips. Brush the strips with some of the butter. Place 1 teaspoon of the cheese mixture at the base of each strip. Fold the corner over to the opposite edge to cover the filling, forming a triangle. Continue folding the strip in a triangular manner until the entire strip is folded, as for a flag. The end result will be a triangle with several layers of wrapped phyllo dough. Arrange on a baking sheet. Repeat the process with the remaining phyllo, most of the remaining butter and the remaining cheese mixture.

Brush the tops of the triangles with the remaining butter. Bake at 375 degrees for 20 minutes or until golden brown and flaky. Serve warm.

*Makes about 100 tiropitas*

*ONE OF OUR FAMILY TRADITIONS IS TO MAKE TIROPITAS, A GREEK HORS D'OEUVRE, EVERY SEASON FOR OUR CHRISTMAS EVE PARTY. THESE TRIANGLES MAY BE ASSEMBLED AHEAD OF TIME AND FROZEN. WHEN READY TO SERVE, SIMPLY TAKE OUT OF THE FREEZER, BRUSH WITH MELTED BUTTER, AND BAKE AS PER INSTRUCTIONS.*

# SLIDERS

*1½ pounds ground sirloin*
*1 large shallot, finely chopped*
*1 tablespoon chopped flat-leaf parsley*
*1 teaspoon salt*
*½ teaspoon pepper*
*¼ cup extra-virgin olive oil*
*Dijon mustard to taste*
*12 soft dinner rolls, split into halves*
*8 ounces Cheddar cheese or Gruyère cheese, shredded*
*Ketchup (optional)*

Combine the ground sirloin, shallot, parsley, salt and pepper in a bowl and mix well. Shape into twelve equal patties.

Heat 2 tablespoons of the olive oil in a large skillet over medium-high heat. Cook six of the patties in the oil for 2 minutes on one side. Turn and cook for 2 minutes longer for medium-rare or to the desired degree of doneness; drain. Heat the remaining 2 tablespoons olive oil in the skillet and repeat the process with the remaining patties.

Spread Dijon mustard on the bottom halves of the rolls and arrange mustard side up on a broiler rack in a broiler pan. Arrange one patty on each roll bottom and top evenly with the cheese. Broil for 30 seconds or until the cheese melts. Drizzle with ketchup and top with the roll tops. Serve immediately.

*Makes 1 dozen*

*This is what we call "man" food at my house! These mini burgers are great with cocktails—very satisfying. Who doesn't love a burger?*

# MARYLAND CRAB CAKES WITH RÉMOULADE DIP

### RÉMOULADE DIP

1 cup mayonnaise

1 hard-cooked egg

1 garlic clove

2 tablespoons minced fresh parsley

1 tablespoon Dijon mustard

1 tablespoon capers

1 teaspoon fresh lemon juice

1 teaspoon dried dill weed

1 teaspoon minced scallion

White pepper or cayenne pepper to taste

### CRAB CAKES

1½ cups unseasoned dry bread crumbs

1½ teaspoons dry mustard

1½ teaspoons Old Bay seasoning

1 egg

½ cup mayonnaise

1 teaspoon lemon juice

1 teaspoon Worcestershire sauce

1 pound fresh lump crab meat, shells
   removed and meat flaked

¼ cup (or more) vegetable oil

To prepare the dip, combine the mayonnaise, egg, garlic, parsley, Dijon mustard, capers, lemon juice, dill weed, scallion and white pepper in a food processor or blender and pulse until combined. Taste and adjust the seasonings. Serve with crudités, shrimp, crab cakes and/or crab legs. You may prepare up to 1 day in advance and store, covered, in the refrigerator.

To prepare the crab cakes, mix the bread crumbs, dry mustard and Old Bay seasoning in a bowl. Whisk the egg in a bowl and stir in the mayonnaise, lemon juice and Worcestershire sauce. Fold in half the bread crumb mixture and the crab meat. Shape by ½ cupfuls into cakes and coat with the remaining bread crumb mixture. Chill, covered, for 2 hours or longer. Heat ¼ cup oil in a heavy skillet until hot. Fry the cakes in batches in the oil for 2 to 3 minutes per side or until golden brown, turning once and adding oil as needed. Drain on paper towels. Serve hot with the dip and lemon wedges.

*Serves 12*

*WE SERVED THESE CRAB CAKES IN OUR FAMILY RESTAURANT. OUR CUSTOMERS LOVED THEM AND ALWAYS COMMENTED ON HOW THEY WERE BURSTING WITH CRAB MEAT—NOT BREADING. YOU CAN USE ½-CUP MEASURE FOR ENTRÉE-SIZE PORTIONS OR GENEROUS TABLESPOON MEASURES FOR MINI CRAB CAKES. THE RÉMOULADE DIP IS A NEVER-FAIL STAPLE THAT CAN BE SERVED WITH ALL VARIETIES OF FISH AND EVEN FRESH STEAMED VEGETABLES. THE PERFECT COMPLEMENT FOR CRAB CAKES.*

# Open House Punch

*1 fifth of Southern Comfort, chilled*
*¾ cup fresh lemon juice, chilled*
*1 (6-ounce) can frozen orange juice concentrate*
*1 (6-ounce) can frozen lemonade concentrate*
*12 cups lemon-lime soda, chilled*
*Red food coloring (optional)*
*1 or 2 lemons, sliced and cut into semicircles*
*1 or 2 oranges, sliced and cut into semicircles*

Combine the liqueur, lemon juice, orange juice concentrate and lemonade concentrate in a large punch bowl and mix well. Stir in the soda. Add food coloring if desired and mix well.

Mix in ice and then the lemon slices and orange slices. Ladle into punch cups. The juice concentrates can be added to the punch bowl frozen and will keep the punch cool during the thawing process.

*Makes 32 (6- to 8-ounce) servings*

*I'm not sure where my parents found this recipe, but it was given to me when my husband and I were hosting our first holiday party together. My parents would serve this punch at their annual Christmas party, and the children were NEVER invited. I distinctly remember being tucked in my bed—hearing them get more and more "festive" as the night went on. Cheers!*

# CHAMPAGNE RASPBERRY PUNCH

*2 cups passion fruit juice or pineapple juice*
*1 cup Triple Sec*
*1 cup brandy*
*½ cup raspberry liqueur*
*2 (750-milliliter) bottles brut Champagne, chilled*
*4 cups ginger ale, chilled*
*1 cup fresh raspberries*

Combine the passion fruit juice, Triple Sec, brandy and raspberry liqueur in a punch bowl and mix well. Chill, covered, for 2 to 10 hours. Stir in the Champagne, ginger ale and raspberries just before serving. Ladle into punch cups.

*Serves 12*

*Lovely looking as well as delicious, this is the perfect cocktail for a shower or brunch. I had this at my sister-in-law's house during a ladies' party years ago and have been making (and drinking it!) ever since.*

# RUBY RED GRAPEFRUIT SPARKLER

*1 cup water*
*1 cup sugar*
*10 star anise*
*8 cups ruby red grapefruit juice, chilled*
*½ cup Campari*
*1 (750-milliliter) bottle Champagne, chilled*

Bring the water, sugar and star anise to a boil in a saucepan and boil until the sugar dissolves, stirring occasionally. Let stand until cool. Strain through a fine sieve into a measuring cup, discarding the star anise. The syrup should measure 1 cup. Chill, covered with plastic wrap, in the refrigerator.

Combine the chilled syrup, grapefruit juice and Campari in a large pitcher and mix well. Divide the grapefruit mixture evenly among glasses and top with the Champagne, stirring well. Serve immediately.

*Serves 8 to 10*

THIS IS AN UNEXPECTED TWIST ON THE TRADITIONAL MIMOSA. THE CAMPARI ADDS AN AMAZING DEEP RED COLOR, AND THE STAR ANISE ADDS AN UNEXPECTED LICORICE FLAVOR. CIN CIN!

# LIMEY APRICOT RUM SLUSHY

*6 tablespoons sugar*

*2 tablespoons freshly grated lime zest (about 6 limes)*

*2 tablespoons fresh lime juice*

*2 cups apricot nectar, chilled*

*2 cups cracked ice*

*1¼ cups white rum*

*¼ cup fresh lime juice*

Combine the sugar and lime zest in a food processor and pulse until finely ground. Reserve ¼ cup of the sugar mixture. Pour the remaining sugar mixture into a shallow dish. Pour 2 tablespoons lime juice into another shallow dish. Dip the rims of four glasses in the juice. Rotate the moist rims gently in the sugar mixture to coat evenly.

Combine the reserved ¼ cup sugar mixture, the apricot nectar, ice, rum and ¼ cup lime juice in a blender and process until puréed. Pour evenly into the prepared glasses and serve immediately.

*Serves 4*

*I SERVE THESE IN THE DEAD OF WINTER TO IMMEDIATELY TRANSPORT MY GUESTS TO THE LAZY DAYS OF SUMMER OR TO AN ISLAND GETAWAY!*

# POMEGRANATE MOJITOS

*¼ cup raw sugar*
*2¼ tablespoons fresh lime juice*
*24 mint leaves*
*¾ cup white rum*
*½ cup pomegranate juice*
*Soda water*

Mix the sugar, lime juice and mint leaves in a bowl. Divide evenly between two tall glasses. Mash the mint mixture with the back of a wooden spoon or a muddler. Mix equal portions of the rum and pomegranate juice in each glass. Fill the glasses with ice and top off with a splash of soda water. Serve immediately.

*Serves 2*

*VIBRANT AND REFRESHING, THESE FESTIVE AND PROFESSIONAL-LOOKING DRINKS ALWAYS SET THE TONE FOR A CHIC AND LIVELY EVENING!*

# FRESH MARGARITAS

*1 lime wedge*
*Salt*
*1 cup tequila*
*1 cup Triple Sec*
*½ cup fresh lime juice*
*½ cup fresh lemon juice*
*2 tablespoons sugar or Splenda*
*Pinch of salt*

Moisten the rims of glasses with a lime wedge and rotate the rims gently in salt, if desired. Combine the tequila, Triple Sec, lime juice, lemon juice, sugar and salt in a pitcher or large cocktail shaker. Stir or shake until combined. Pour over ice in the prepared glasses and garnish with lime wedges. For frozen margaritas, process all the ingredients with 2 cups ice in a blender to the desired consistency.

*Serves 4 to 6*

THE STORY BEHIND THIS RECIPE INVOLVES A NERVOUS BABY-SITTING FATHER OF TWO, HIS WIFE, A MARGARITA-TOTING WOMAN TALKING ON HER CELL PHONE WHILE DRIVING, AND A POLICE OFFICER. THE END RESULT? ONE HAPPY FATHER AND A MARGARITA RECIPE SURE TO CURE ANYONE'S CASE OF THE NERVES.

# Spicy Bloody Marys

*Vodka to taste*
*2 (32-ounce) cans tomato juice*
*3 tablespoons prepared horseradish*
*2 tablespoons Worcestershire sauce*
*2 tablespoons clam juice*
*2 tablespoons chopped fresh cilantro*
*1 tablespoon fresh lime juice*
*Hot and/or smoky red pepper sauce to taste*
*Celery salt to taste*
*Freshly ground pepper to taste*
*Chili powder to taste*

Chill the vodka in the freezer. Process the tomato juice, horseradish, Worcestershire sauce, clam juice, cilantro, lime juice, hot sauce, celery salt, pepper and chili powder in a food processor or blender to the desired consistency. Fill an ice cube tray with a small amount of the Bloody Mary mixture and freeze. Pour the remaining Bloody Mary mixture into a pitcher and chill, covered, for 8 to 10 hours.

Pour the chilled Bloody Mary mix into tall glasses and add the desired amount of vodka. Garnish with lime wedges, celery ribs, pickle spears, skewered olives and/or Bloody Mary ice cubes. Serve immediately.

*Serves 8*

*THIS IS MY HUSBAND'S OWN RECIPE THAT HAS EVOLVED FROM HIS COLLEGE DAYS TO THE PRESENT DAY. ON OUR HONEYMOON WE HAD BLOODY MARYS AT THE RITZ IN MADRID AND WERE INSPIRED BY HOW ELEGANT THEY LOOKED WITHOUT ICE AND THEY NEVER GOT WATERY!*

# Southsiders

*½ cup vodka*
*1 cup fresh lemonade with pulp*
*½ cup soda water*
*Fresh mint*

Fill two tall glasses with ice cubes. Pour equal amounts of the vodka and lemonade into the glasses. Top off each with the soda water and then stir. Garnish with sprigs of mint. Serve immediately.

*Serves 2*

*THIS DRINK IS SO LIGHT AND REFRESHING ON A HOT SUMMER DAY; WE LOVE TO SIT ON OUR PATIO AND ENJOY A "GROWN-UP" LEMONADE!*

# WHITE SANGRIA

*2 (750-milliliter) bottles dry white wine*
*1 cup orange juice*
*¾ cup brandy*
*½ cup Triple Sec*
*¾ cup simple syrup*
*¾ cup passion fruit purée*
*1 orange or blood orange, sliced and cut into thin semicircles*
*1 lemon, sliced and cut into thin semicircles*
*½ to 1 pint fresh blackberries*

Prepare simple syrup by combining equal portions of sugar and water in a saucepan. Cook over low heat until the sugar dissolves and then boil for 1 minute. Pour into a bowl and chill.

Combine the wine, orange juice, brandy, Triple Sec, simple syrup, passion fruit purée, orange slices, lemon slices and blackberries in a large pitcher and mix well. Chill, covered, for 2 to 48 hours. Pour the sangria and fruit over ice in glasses. Serve immediately.

*Serves 10*

*I FIRST MADE THIS FOR THE PARENTS' COMMITTEE AT MY DAUGHTER'S NURSERY SCHOOL. IT IS NOW A STAPLE AT ALL OF OUR FUNCTIONS. PRESCHOOL WAS NEVER SO MUCH FUN!*

# LONG ISLAND GREEN TEA

½ cup superfine sugar

½ cup hot water

1 cup fresh lemon juice

1 (750-milliliter) bottle sake

10 bags green tea

⅔ cup lemon vodka

⅔ cup gin

4 teaspoons grenadine

Dissolve the sugar in the hot water in a heatproof bowl and stir in the lemon juice. Chill the sour mix in the refrigerator. Immerse the sake bottle in a large bowl of hot water and let stand for 15 minutes. Pour the sake into a bowl and add the tea bags. Steep for 40 minutes.

Strain the sake mixture into a pitcher, discarding the tea bags. Stir in the chilled sour mix, vodka and gin.

Pour equally into ice-filled glasses and add 1 teaspoon of the grenadine to each glass. Mix well and serve immediately.

*Serves 4*

*THIS UPDATED CLASSIC SHOULD COME WITH A WARNING SIGN: DRINKER BEWARE. POTENT, EXOTIC, AND DELICIOUS—ALWAYS A HIT.*

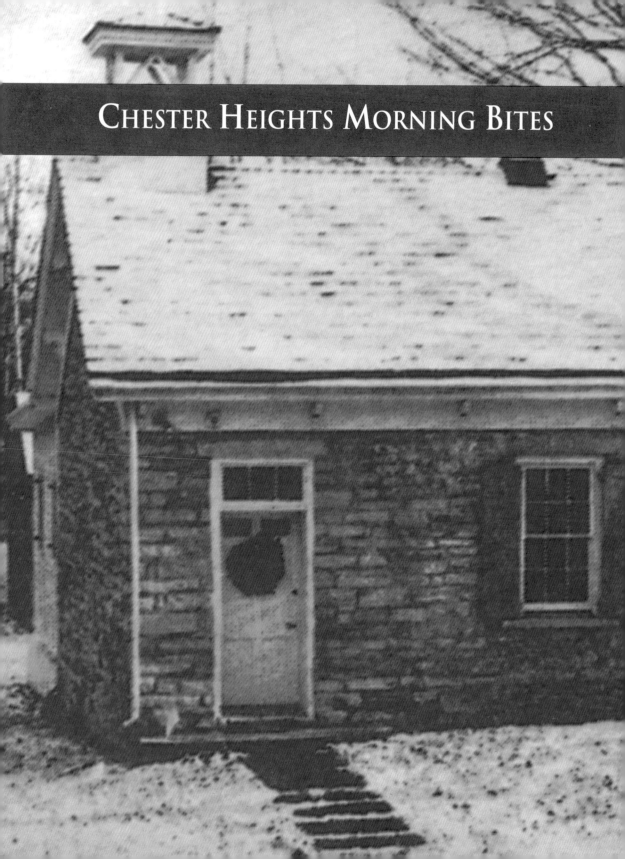

# Eastchester, New York

*"Chester Heights Morning Bites"*

*The Chester Heights section of Eastchester is where the famous
Marble School House, built in 1835, is located.*

Originally the home to the Siwanoy Indian tribe, the town of Eastchester is most notable for its residents' contribution to the development of the freedom of religion and the freedom of the press in this country, thus earning its name as the "Birthplace of the Bill of Rights."

As an early feminist leader and strong advocate for religious freedom, Anne Hutchinson settled in the area in 1642, long before Eastchester was formally established. Soon after, she and her family met their fate at the hands of the Siwanoy Indian tribe in 1643.

In 1733 an incident occurred on the village green when John Peter Zenger, a reporter for the *New York Journal* who was covering the account of an election held at St. Paul's Church in Eastchester, criticized the governor's conduct. Zenger was arrested and tried for seditious libel. He was acquitted in 1735, after a one-day trial. His lawyer, Alexander Hamilton, argued that mere publication did not constitute libel, but that falsehood had to be proved. This moment established the legal precedent for "freedom of the press" and was later incorporated as a basic freedom in the Bill of Rights.

Eastchester became a township in 1788, which at the time included present-day Eastchester, the villages of Bronxville and Tuckahoe, all of Mount Vernon, and a good portion of the Bronx.

In 1974 The Junior League of Bronxville was instrumental in creating the first community-wide recycling program in Eastchester called RECYCLE! The JLB has also worked with the Family Consultation Services of Eastchester and the Eastchester Child Development Center. Most recently, in the wake of September 11, 2001, The Junior League of Bronxville was instrumental in the development of the Eastchester Citizens Corps, a group of volunteers trained to assist individuals, as well as emergency service providers, during local or national disasters.

## Chester Heights Morning Bites
# Brunch and Breads

Homemade Granola
Artichoke, Mushroom and Spinach Frittata
Goat Cheese and Leek Tart
Rebel Eggs
Baked French Toast
Pancakes
Fresh Fruit with Ginger and Mint
Chocolate Croissant Bread Pudding

❧❧

Holiday Sing Coffee Cake
Banana Mango Bread
Zucchini and Roasted Sweet Potato Bread
French Doughnuts
Miniature Jalapeño Muffins

# HOMEMADE GRANOLA

*4 cups rolled oats*

*2 cups sweetened shredded coconut*

*2 cups sliced raw almonds (do not use roasted)*

*¾ cup vegetable oil or canola oil*

*½ cup honey*

*1½ cups dried apricots, peaches or plums, chopped*

*1 cup golden raisins*

*1 cup dried cherries*

*1 cup dried cranberries*

*1 cup whole or chopped unsalted roasted cashews*

Toss the oats, coconut and almonds in a large bowl. Whisk the oil and honey in a bowl until blended. Pour over the oat mixture and stir with a wooden spoon to coat. Spread on a nonstick baking sheet.

Bake at 350 degrees for 15 to 45 minutes or until golden brown, stirring occasionally with a spatula. Let stand until cool and then stir.

Combine the oat mixture, apricots, raisins, cherries, cranberries and cashews in a bowl and mix well. Serve with vanilla yogurt or pour milk over the granola in a bowl. Store in an airtight container for up to 1 week.

*Serves 15*

*I ALWAYS MAKE THIS GRANOLA WHEN I AM HOSTING A BRUNCH. GROWN-UPS AND KIDS LOVE IT! YOU CAN USE ANY DRIED FRUITS THAT YOU AND YOUR FAMILY LIKE, SO IT CAN BE CUSTOMIZED TO YOUR PERSONAL TASTES!*

# Artichoke, Mushroom and Spinach Frittata

*1 (10-ounce) package frozen chopped*
   *spinach, thawed and drained, or*
   *12 ounces fresh spinach, chopped*
*6 ounces sharp Cheddar cheese, Gruyère*
   *cheese, Jarlsberg cheese or fontina*
   *cheese, shredded*
*6 eggs*
*2 tablespoons milk or water*

*Salt and pepper to taste*
*Few dashes of Tabasco sauce (optional)*
*3 tablespoons olive oil*
*8 ounces cremini mushrooms, thinly sliced*
*1 onion, cut into halves and thinly sliced*
*1 (12-ounce) jar marinated artichoke*
   *hearts, drained and thinly sliced*

Press any excess moisture from the frozen spinach. Whisk the cheese, eggs, milk, salt, pepper and Tabasco sauce in a bowl until combined.

Heat the olive oil in a 10- to 12-inch ovenproof skillet over medium heat. Sauté the mushrooms in the oil for 3 minutes or until they begin to soften. Stir in the onion and cook for 5 to 7 minutes or until the mushrooms and onion are very tender. Add the frozen spinach and stir until combined. If using fresh spinach, cover the skillet and cook for 3 minutes or until the spinach wilts. Stir in the artichokes and pat the mixture down. Reduce the heat to medium-low.

Pour the egg mixture over the vegetables and stir gently. Cook for 3 minutes or until the bottom is set, lifting the edge of the frittata and tilting the skillet to allow the uncooked egg to flow to the bottom. Bake, covered, at 350 degrees for 12 to 15 minutes or to the desired degree of doneness. Slice into wedges and serve immediately.

*Serves 6*

*The first time I had this at my friend's house for brunch, I had to have the recipe! It is easier than an omelet and makes an appealing and impressive presentation.*

# GOAT CHEESE AND LEEK TART

*1 unbaked (9-inch) pie shell*
*3 or 4 leeks*
*2 tablespoons olive oil*
*2 tablespoons heavy cream*
*1/2 teaspoon salt*
*1/4 teaspoon pepper*
*1 1/2 tablespoons chopped fresh tarragon*
*4 ounces goat cheese, crumbled*

Prick the bottom of the pie shell with a fork. Bake at 425 degrees for 8 to 10 minutes or use the package directions. Let cool on a wire rack. Reduce the oven temperature to 375 degrees.

Remove the root, tough outer leaves and tops from the leeks, leaving 2 inches of the dark leaves. Thinly slice the leeks. Rinse and pat dry with paper towels. Sauté the leeks in the olive oil in a skillet over medium heat for 8 to 10 minutes or until tender but not brown. Stir in the cream, salt and pepper. Cook for 4 to 5 minutes or until slightly thickened, stirring constantly. Add the tarragon and mix well.

Sprinkle half the cheese over the bottom of the pie shell and top with the leek mixture. Sprinkle with the remaining cheese. Bake for 18 to 20 minutes or until golden brown and bubbly. Serve warm.

*Serves 4*

*I MADE THIS FOR A BOOK CLUB DINNER AND THEN BEGAN TAKING IT TO FAMILIES WITH NEW BABIES. IN THE NINTH MONTH AND COUNTING, MY FRIENDS TOOK TO "RESERVING" THIS DISH.*

# REBEL EGGS

1 pound sweet Italian pork sausage or
    chicken sausage, casings removed
2 cups milk
6 eggs
1 teaspoon dry mustard
1 tablespoon butter
6 slices white or multigrain bread, cut into pieces
1 cup (4 ounces) shredded Cheddar cheese

Brown the sausage in a skillet, stirring until crumbly; drain. Whisk the milk, eggs and dry mustard in a bowl until blended.

Coat the bottom and sides of a 9×13-inch baking pan with the butter. Layer the bread, cheese and sausage in the prepared pan. Pour the egg mixture over the prepared layers. Chill, covered, for 8 hours to overnight. Bake, uncovered, at 350 degrees for 40 to 50 minutes or until set. Serve hot.

*Serves 6 to 8*

THE SAME SOUTHERN MINDSET THAT INSPIRED SCARLETT O'HARA TO MAKE A GOWN FROM A PAIR OF VELVET DRAPES INSPIRED MY SORORITY SISTERS TO MAKE THIS DISH. REBEL EGGS WAS A DELICIOUS WAY FOR US TO TAKE A FEW EGGS AND FEED A HUNGRY CROWD A DELICIOUS BREAKFAST!

# Baked French Toast

1 cup packed light brown sugar
½ cup light corn syrup
¼ cup (½ stick) unsalted butter, melted
1 loaf French bread, cut diagonally into 1-inch slices
2½ cups 2% milk
3 eggs
1 tablespoon all-purpose flour
1½ teaspoons vanilla extract
¼ teaspoon salt
3 tablespoons granulated sugar
1½ teaspoons cinnamon

Combine the brown sugar, corn syrup and butter in a saucepan. Cook over medium heat for 5 minutes or until bubbly, stirring constantly. Pour into a 9×13-inch baking dish sprayed with nonstick cooking spray. Arrange the bread slices in a single layer in the prepared pan; they will be crowded.

Whisk the milk, eggs, flour, vanilla and salt in a bowl until blended. Pour over the bread slices. Chill, covered, for 8 hours to overnight. Mix the granulated sugar and cinnamon in a bowl and sprinkle over the top. Bake at 350 degrees for 50 minutes or until golden brown and puffed. Let stand for 5 minutes before serving.

*Serves 10*

*This is a completely crave worthy dish, and the above recipe is the "lightened" version!*
*I make it every year to serve for Christmas Eve brunch, and it is always very happily received.*

# PANCAKES

*1½ cups all-purpose flour*
*2 tablespoons sugar*
*2 tablespoons malted milk powder (optional)*
*2 teaspoons baking powder*
*¾ teaspoon salt*
*1¼ cups milk*
*2 eggs*
*2 teaspoons vanilla extract*
*3 tablespoons vegetable oil or canola oil*
*Berries, chocolate chips or toppings of choice (optional)*

Whisk the flour, sugar, malted milk powder (if using), baking powder and salt in a bowl until combined. Combine the milk, eggs and vanilla in a mixing bowl or blender and beat or process at high speed for 3 minutes or until light and foamy.

Pour into a bowl and stir in the oil. Add the dry ingredients and mix gently. Let the batter stand to thicken while the griddle is heating or store, covered, in the refrigerator for 8 hours to overnight.

Pour ¼ cupful of the batter onto a hot lightly greased griddle. Cook until bubbles appear on the surface and begin to break; add berries, chocolate chips or toppings of choice. Turn the pancake and cook until the remaining side is brown. Repeat the process with the remaining batter.

*Serves 4 to 6*

THIS IS MY HUSBAND'S RECIPE. HE IS KNOWN AS THE KING OF BREAKFAST IN OUR HOUSE. HE TELLS THE KIDS THAT THE VANILLA IS HIS SECRET INGREDIENT AND THEY ARE TO KEEP IT HUSH HUSH. ADDING IN BERRIES OR EVEN A FEW CHOCOLATE CHIPS LETS EVERYONE FEEL LIKE THE MASTER CHEF!

# Fresh Fruit with Ginger and Mint

### Ginger Syrup

*3 cups water*

*2 cups sugar*

*½ cup thinly sliced unpeeled fresh ginger (about 8 ounces)*

### Fruit Salad

*4 cups (1-inch) pieces fresh fruit, such as berries, melon and mangoes*

*3 tablespoons fresh mint, cut into shreds*

To prepare the syrup, bring the water, sugar and ginger to a boil in a 2-quart saucepan and boil until the sugar dissolves, stirring frequently. Reduce the heat and simmer for 10 minutes, stirring occasionally. Let steep for 15 minutes. Strain the syrup into a bowl, discarding the ginger. Chill, covered, for 2 hours or longer.

To prepare the fruit, toss the fresh fruit with the mint in a bowl. Add one-fourth of the chilled syrup, or more to taste, and mix well. Serve immediately.

*Serves 4 to 6*

*In the summer my mother often serves lunch on her elegant front porch. This is one of her favorite dishes to enjoy there.*

# CHOCOLATE CROISSANT BREAD PUDDING

*6 to 6½ cups lightly packed bite-size pieces croissant*
*(about 6 croissants)*
*6 ounces bittersweet or semisweet chocolate, chopped*
*(do not use chocolate chips)*
*1¼ cups heavy cream*
*1¼ cups milk*
*½ cup sugar*
*2 eggs*
*2 egg yolks*
*2 teaspoons vanilla extract*

Arrange the croissant pieces in a buttered 9×13-inch baking dish. Sprinkle the chocolate over the top. Whisk the cream, milk, sugar, eggs, egg yolks and vanilla in a bowl until blended.

Pour the custard over the prepared layers and pat lightly to ensure the bread is immersed in the custard. Let stand for 5 to 10 minutes. Stir and pat down again, keeping the chocolate well distributed. Some of the bread will remain above the custard.

Bake at 350 degrees for about 35 minutes or until golden brown and slightly puffed. Serve warm.

*Serves 6 to 8*

*THIS RICH DECADENT BREAKFAST TREAT REMINDS ME OF A DELICIOUS FRENCH PAIN AU CHOCOLAT. INDULGE YOUR FAVORITE CHOCOHOLIC!*

# HOLIDAY SING COFFEE CAKE

1½ cups walnuts, finely chopped

1½ cups packed light brown sugar

1½ tablespoons cinnamon

1½ tablespoons baking cocoa

¾ cup (1½ sticks) unsalted butter, softened

1½ cups granulated sugar

3 eggs

1½ tablespoons vanilla extract

1½ teaspoons baking soda

1½ teaspoons baking powder

¾ teaspoon salt

3 cups all-purpose flour

2 cups reduced-fat sour cream

1 cup confectioners' sugar, sifted

1 to 2 tablespoons milk

Grease a 12-cup bundt pan or spray with nonstick cooking spray. Mix the walnuts, brown sugar, cinnamon and baking cocoa in a bowl. Beat the butter and granulated sugar in a mixing bowl until light and fluffy, scraping the bowl occasionally. Add the eggs one at a time, beating well after each addition. Blend in the vanilla. Add the baking soda, baking powder and salt and mix until blended. Add the flour and sour cream alternately, mixing well after each addition.

Spread one-third of the batter in the prepared pan and sprinkle with half the walnut mixture. Layer with half the remaining batter, the remaining walnut mixture and the remaining batter.

Bake at 350 degrees for 1 hour or until a knife inserted near the center comes out clean. Cool in the pan for 10 minutes. Remove to a wire rack to cool completely. Whisk the confectioners' sugar and milk in a bowl until of a glaze consistency and drizzle over the top of the coffee cake.

*Serves 12*

*I BROUGHT THIS COFFEE CAKE TO MY DAUGHTER'S FIRST HOLIDAY SING BREAKFAST AT HER ELEMENTARY SCHOOL. ONE DAD ASKED ME IF I WAS MARRIED. NOW I AM ASKED TO BRING IT EVERY YEAR. THE NUT MIXTURE WILL YIELD ENOUGH FOR TWO GOOD-SIZE RIBBONS OF STREUSEL—DON'T HOLD BACK ON USING ALL OF THE NUT MIXTURE IN THE CAKE.*

# Banana Mango Bread

2 cups sifted all-purpose flour
2 teaspoons baking soda
2 teaspoons cinnamon
1 teaspoon nutmeg
1 teaspoon salt
1 cup granulated sugar
1 cup packed dark brown sugar

1 cup vegetable oil
3 eggs, lightly beaten
2 cups mashed mangoes
1 cup raisins
1 cup chopped walnuts
2 ripe bananas, mashed
1 cup sweetened shredded coconut

Sift the flour, baking soda, cinnamon, nutmeg and salt into a mixing bowl and mix well. Make a well in the flour mixture and add the granulated sugar, brown sugar, oil and eggs to the well. Beat until combined. Fold in the mangoes, raisins, walnuts and bananas.

Spoon equal portions of the batter into two greased and floured loaf pans. Sprinkle the coconut over the top. Bake at 350 degrees for 50 to 60 minutes or until a knife inserted in the centers comes out clean. Cool in the pans for 10 minutes. Remove to a wire rack to cool completely. Wrap in foil to store.

*Makes 2 loaves*

AS A MIAMI NATIVE WE ALWAYS HAD FAR TOO MANY MANGOES. THIS HAS BECOME A CHRISTMAS GIFT TRADITION HERE IN NEW YORK. IT IS GREAT SLICED AND TOASTED, TOO.

# ZUCCHINI AND ROASTED SWEET POTATO BREAD

3½ cups all-purpose flour
1½ teaspoons baking soda
1 teaspoon baking powder
1 teaspoon salt
1 teaspoon cinnamon
½ teaspoon nutmeg
½ teaspoon ginger

4 eggs
1¾ cups sugar
1 cup vegetable oil
1 sweet potato, roasted, peeled and mashed
2 cups grated zucchini
2 teaspoons vanilla extract

Mix the flour, baking soda, baking powder, salt, cinnamon, nutmeg and ginger in a bowl. Beat the eggs in a mixing bowl until blended. Add the sugar gradually, beating constantly until combined. Add the oil and sweet potato and mix well. Add the flour mixture and zucchini alternately, mixing well after each addition. Blend in the vanilla.

Spoon the batter evenly into two greased and floured loaf pans. Bake at 350 degrees for 55 to 60 minutes or until a wooden pick inserted in the centers comes out clean. Cool in the pans for 10 minutes. Remove to a wire rack to cool completely.

*Makes 2 loaves*

*HONESTLY, MY KIDS LOVE THIS AND HAVE NO IDEA THAT IT'S GOOD FOR THEM. TIP: THE RECIPE MAKES TWO LOAVES, AND THE SECOND FREEZES BEAUTIFULLY.*

# FRENCH DOUGHNUTS

*1½ cups all-purpose flour*
*½ cup sugar*
*2 teaspoons baking powder*
*¼ teaspoon salt*
*¼ teaspoon nutmeg*
*½ cup milk*
*1 egg, lightly beaten*
*⅓ cup unsalted butter, melted*
*½ teaspoon vanilla extract*
*½ cup sugar*
*1 teaspoon cinnamon*
*¼ cup (½ stick) unsalted butter, melted*

Sift the flour, ½ cup sugar, the baking powder, salt and nutmeg into a bowl and mix well. Combine the milk, egg, ⅓ cup butter and the vanilla in a bowl and mix well. Add to the flour mixture and stir just until moistened. Fill buttered muffin cups one-half full. Bake at 400 degrees for 20 minutes.

Mix ½ cup sugar and the cinnamon in a shallow dish. Remove the hot doughnuts from the pan immediately and brush with ¼ cup butter. Roll in the cinnamon-sugar to coat. Serve warm.

*Serves 6*

*MY MOTHER MADE THESE FLUFFY BAKED DOUGHNUTS FOR ME AND MY SISTERS WHEN WE WERE CHILDREN. NOW, I LOVE THEM WITH COFFEE!*

# MINIATURE JALAPEÑO MUFFINS

*1½ cups yellow cornmeal*
*1 tablespoon baking powder*
*½ teaspoon salt*
*¼ teaspoon freshly ground pepper*
*1 cup (4 ounces) shredded sharp Cheddar cheese*
*1 cup grated onion*
*5 large jalapeño chiles, finely chopped*
*1 (8-ounce) can cream-style corn*
*1 cup sour cream*
*½ cup corn oil*
*3 eggs, lightly beaten*

Combine the cornmeal, baking powder, salt and pepper in a bowl and mix well. Stir in the cheese, onion and chiles. Add the corn, sour cream, corn oil and eggs and mix just until moistened.

Spoon the batter evenly into buttered miniature muffin cups. Bake at 400 degrees for 10 to 15 minutes or until a wooden pick inserted in the centers comes out clean.

*Makes 10 to 12 miniature muffins*

*I ALWAYS MAKE THESE WHEN WE ARE HAVING A SOUTHWESTERN-INFLUENCED MEAL SUCH AS ENCHILADAS, FAJITAS, OR TACOS. THEY ARE TRULY ADDICTIVE.*

# HEARTY HILLTOP FARE

# BRONXVILLE, NEW YORK

*"Hearty Hilltop Fare"*

*Historic Sagamore Park, once an artists' colony, is now more commonly referred to as "the Hilltop."*

Bronxville, New York, is a charming English-style village located fifteen miles north of midtown Manhattan, nestled along the banks of the Bronx River in Southern Westchester County, New York. Originally known as Underhill's Crossing, the Village took the name of Bronxville and in 1898 was incorporated within the town of Eastchester.

At the turn of the century, a thriving artists' colony was established on Sunset Hill, the site where Gramatan, Chief of the Mohicans, signed a deed transferring the area to western settlers in 1666. The area, known today simply as "the Hilltop," was also home to the Hotel Gramatan, which dominated the skyline from 1905 to its demolition in 1972.

Evolving from a tiny settlement of farm, orchard, estate, and factory land, Bronxville has become one of the nation's premier metropolitan suburbs, at just one square mile in total area. A city planner's dream, of a pedestrian scale, a mix of multifamily and single-family housing, all located around a central business district, Bronxville is a suburb that many have tried to duplicate, but have not succeeded in replicating. While being in such close proximity to the business and cultural center of the world, Bronxville is just a twenty-eight-minute ride to Grand Central Station in New York City.

Having their start in Bronxville, The Junior League of Bronxville has been successful in developing many projects in the area. From initiating the Lawrence Hospital Library Cart, Gift Shop, and Information Desk to Family University, a program dealing with issues facing youth, The Junior League of Bronxville has continued to evolve and grow.

PHOTO: SAGAMORE PARK GATEWAY

HEARTY HILLTOP FARE
# SOUPS AND STEWS

QUICK CHICKEN NOODLE SOUP
TORTILLA SOUP
CREAMY ARTICHOKE SOUP
RED CURRY CARROT SOUP
LENTIL AND RICE SOUP
WILD MUSHROOM SOUP
BUTTERNUT SQUASH APPLE SOUP

BEEF BUDAPEST
CHILI STEW
TURKEY CHILI
IRISH STEW

# Quick Chicken Noodle Soup

*1 tablespoon olive oil*
*3 carrots, peeled and sliced*
*2 ribs celery, sliced*
*1 Spanish onion, chopped*
*1 pound boneless skinless chicken breasts, cut into chunks*
*4 cups chicken broth*
*Sprigs of thyme*
*Salt and pepper to taste*
*6 to 8 ounces wide egg noodles*

Heat the olive oil in a Dutch oven over medium-high heat and add the carrots, celery and onion. Cook for 20 minutes or until the vegetables turn a deep rich color and become sweet. Add the chicken, broth and thyme and mix well. Bring to a boil and reduce the heat.

Simmer until the chicken is cooked through, stirring occasionally. Season with salt and pepper. Add the pasta and cook using the package directions until tender. Ladle into soup bowls. The soup mixture may be frozen before the pasta is added.

*Serves 4 to 6*

*My kids love this simple and perfectly seasoned soup. Forget cooking for hours—this beats a can any day!*

# TORTILLA SOUP

2 poblano chiles
2 (14-ounce) cans whole, peeled tomatoes
1 onion, chopped
¼ cup minced cilantro
2 garlic cloves
2 teaspoons salt
1 teaspoon sugar
4 cups chicken broth
1 pound boneless skinless chicken breasts,
    cut into strips

1 cup sour cream
2 teaspoons minced canned chipotle chiles
    in adobo sauce
3 to 4 cups (12 to 16 ounces) shredded
    Chihuahua cheese, mild Cheddar cheese
    or Monterey Jack cheese
Broken tortilla chips
Chopped avocados

Roast the poblano chiles over the flame of a gas burner until charred, turning frequently. Place in a bowl and cover with plastic wrap. Let stand for 10 minutes or until cool. Remove and discard the charred skins.

Combine the poblano chiles, tomatoes, onion, cilantro, garlic, salt and sugar in a blender or food processor and process until almost smooth. Combine the poblano chile mixture, broth, chicken, sour cream and chipotle chiles in a large stockpot and mix well. Bring to a boil and reduce the heat.

Simmer, covered, for 15 minutes or until the chicken is cooked through, stirring occasionally. Remove the chicken to a cutting board using a slotted spoon. Finely chop the chicken and return to the stockpot. Stir in the cheese. Ladle the soup over broken tortilla chips and chopped avocados in soup bowls. Serve with lime wedges.

*Serves 8 to 10*

THIS IS ONE OF THE FEW SOUPS I MAKE THAT BOTH MY CHILDREN AND HUSBAND TRULY LOVE.
THE KIDS LOOK FORWARD TO THE ADDED TORTILLA CHIPS!

# CREAMY ARTICHOKE SOUP

   *3 tablespoons olive oil*
   *4 leek bulbs, sliced*
   *1 garlic clove, minced*
   *2 baking potatoes, peeled and chopped*
   *6 cups chicken stock*
   *2 (14-ounce) can artichoke hearts, drained and coarsely chopped*
   *1 teaspoon salt*
   *Pepper to taste*
   *1 tablespoon lemon juice*
   *Crème fraîche*
   *Chopped fresh chives*

Heat the olive oil in a large stockpot over medium heat and add the leeks and garlic. Cook until the leeks are tender; do not allow the garlic to burn. Stir in the potatoes. Cook for about 5 minutes, stirring constantly. Add the stock, artichokes, salt and pepper and mix well.

Cook for about 25 minutes or until the vegetables are tender. Purée the soup using an immersion blender or purée in batches in a blender. Stir in the lemon juice. Ladle into soup bowls and garnish each serving with a dollop of crème fraîche and a sprinkling of chopped fresh chives.

*Serves 6 to 8*

*THIS VERSATILE SOUP IS EQUALLY ELEGANT AND SATISFYING TO A HUNGRY CROWD. I'VE SERVED THIS TO GUESTS GATHERED FOR SUNDAY FOOTBALL——IN A BOWL ON THEIR LAPS WITHOUT THE GARNISH——AS WELL AS FOR A FIRST COURSE AT FORMAL DINNER PARTIES.*

# RED CURRY CARROT SOUP

2 tablespoons vegetable oil
6 large carrots, peeled and cut into
    2-inch chunks
1 (½-inch) piece fresh ginger, peeled
1 Vidalia onion or sweet onion, chopped
6 cups chicken stock
½ cup unsweetened coconut milk

1 teaspoon red curry paste
Salt and pepper to taste
2 tablespoons fresh cilantro, chopped
1 tablespoon fresh basil, chopped
1 tablespoon fresh mint, chopped
1 scallion, chopped
Fresh lime juice to taste

Heat the oil in a stockpot and add the carrots and ginger. Cook until the carrots are light brown, stirring constantly. Add the onion and cook for 2 minutes or until tender. Stir in the stock, coconut milk and curry paste. Bring to a boil and reduce the heat.

Simmer over medium heat for 25 minutes. Strain, reserving the cooking liquid and the solids. Combine the reserved solids with 1 cup or more of the reserved cooking liquid and process until puréed. Mix the purée with the remaining reserved cooking liquid in the stockpot and season with salt and pepper.

Simmer until heated through. Ladle into soup bowls and sprinkle evenly with the cilantro, basil, mint and scallion. Drizzle with lime juice.

*Serves 4 to 6*

THIS SOUP CAN BE SERVED HOT OR CHILLED. YOU WILL BE AMAZED AT HOW THE DELICACY OF THE CARROTS AND THE SPICY PUNCH OF THE RED CURRY COMPLEMENT EACH OTHER. THE COLOR AND TEXTURE OF THIS SOUP IS GORGEOUS, TOO! BE CAREFUL WHEN ADDING THE RED CURRY PASTE—IT IS VERY POTENT AND A LITTLE GOES A LONG WAY.

# LENTIL AND RICE SOUP

*4 ounces pancetta, finely chopped*
*½ cup minced onion*
*2 garlic cloves, minced*
*2 tablespoons chopped parsley*
*Olive oil*
*2 cups chopped canned plum tomatoes with juice*
*1½ cups lentils, rinsed and drained*
*6 cups beef broth*
*3 cups water*
*½ cup arborio rice*
*Salt and pepper to taste*
*Grated Parmesan cheese*

Cook the pancetta, onion, garlic and parsley in olive oil in a stockpot until the pancetta and onion are golden brown, stirring frequently. Stir in the tomatoes and lentils and cook for 5 minutes. Add the broth, water and rice and bring to a boil.

Boil gently for 45 minutes or until the rice is tender, stirring occasionally. Season with salt and pepper and ladle into soup bowls. Serve with grated Parmesan cheese.

*Serves 6 to 8*

*I tasted this at my friend's house when she lived in Bronxville and immediately wrote down the recipe. It is hearty enough to serve for dinner and tastes even more full-flavored the next day.*

# WILD MUSHROOM SOUP

1 cup light cream
1 tablespoon chopped fresh tarragon
Salt and freshly ground pepper to taste
3 leeks
5 tablespoons unsalted butter
12 shallots, sliced
1 pound assorted wild mushrooms, thinly
    sliced (chanterelles, oyster, hen of the
    woods and/or shiitake mushrooms)

12 ounces button mushrooms, sliced
1 cup all-purpose flour
5 cups beef stock
5 cups chicken stock
1 tablespoon chopped fresh tarragon
⅓ cup brandy

Beat the cream in a mixing bowl until soft peaks form. Fold in 1 tablespoon tarragon with a rubber spatula and season with salt and pepper. Chill, covered, until serving time.

Cut the leek bulbs and 1 inch of the tops lengthwise into halves and rinse; slice crosswise. Melt the butter in a large heavy saucepan and add the leeks and shallots. Sauté for 15 minutes or until golden brown. Stir in the mushrooms and sauté for 7 minutes. Add the flour and cook for 3 minutes or until the flour is incorporated, stirring constantly.

Add the beef stock and chicken stock gradually, stirring constantly until combined. Add 1 tablespoon tarragon and bring to a boil, stirring constantly. Reduce the heat to medium-low and simmer for 20 minutes. Season with salt and pepper.

If making ahead, remove from the heat and chill. Just before serving reheat the soup and stir in the brandy. Ladle into soup bowls and top each serving with a generous spoonful of the tarragon cream. Serve immediately.

*Serves 8*

*My girlfriend brought this glorious soup to a potluck dinner and it was the star of the party! You can serve with or without the cream garnish, but the tarragon pulls it all together and adds just the right touch.*

# Butternut Squash Apple Soup

*1 butternut squash*
*3 tablespoons olive oil*
*1 Granny Smith apple, sliced*
*½ large Spanish onion, sliced*
*Salt and pepper to taste*
*4 cups (about) chicken broth*

Cut the squash lengthwise into halves and remove the seeds. Arrange the squash cut side down in a large roasting pan. Pour enough boiling water into the pan to reach halfway up the sides of the squash. Roast at 400 degrees for 45 minutes or until the squash is tender. Let stand until cool and then scoop the pulp into a bowl.

Heat the olive oil in a large skillet and add the apple and onion. Sauté until caramelized and golden brown. Season with salt and pepper. Let stand until cool.

Combine ½ cup of the squash pulp and half the onion mixture in a blender. Add 1 cup of the broth and process until smooth. Pour into a saucepan. Repeat the process with the remaining squash pulp, remaining onion mixture and 1 cup or more of the remaining broth, depending on the desired consistency. Taste and adjust the seasonings and simmer until heated through. Ladle into soup bowls.

*Serves 4 to 6*

*This streamlined soup was a Thanksgiving staple at my family's restaurant and comes together quickly in a blender. Quantities can easily be increased to feed a crowd.*

# BEEF BUDAPEST

*2 tablespoons all-purpose flour*
*Kosher salt and pepper to taste*
*1 pound beef stew meat, cut into pieces*
*2 tablespoons vegetable oil*
*4 ounces mushrooms*
*1 onion, chopped*
*1 garlic clove, minced*
*2 cups water*
*2 (8-ounce) cans tomato sauce*
*1 teaspoon salt*
*1 cup (or more) sour cream*
*16 ounces egg noodles, cooked*

Mix the flour with kosher salt and pepper to taste in a shallow dish. Coat the beef with the flour mixture. Heat the oil in a large saucepan or Dutch oven. Brown the beef in the oil, turning frequently. Add the mushrooms, onion and garlic and sauté lightly. Stir in the water, tomato sauce and 1 teaspoon salt.

Simmer, covered, for 2 hours or until the beef is tender, stirring occasionally. You may freeze at this point for future use, if desired. Add the sour cream and simmer just until heated through; do not boil. Spoon over the hot pasta on a serving platter.

*Serves 6*

THIS RECIPE CAME FROM MY MATERNAL GRANDMOTHER WHOM I CALLED NANA BANANA. SHE WAS THOUGHTFUL AND A PLEASURE TO BE AROUND. JUST THE SMELL OF THIS DISH BRINGS BACK A FLOOD OF MEMORIES OF HER THROUGHOUT MY CHILDHOOD.

# CHILI STEW

1 pound sliced bacon, cut into
  ¼-inch pieces
1½ pounds beef chuck roast, cut into
  2-inch pieces
1½ pounds boneless pork shoulder, cut into
  2-inch pieces
1½ pounds sweet Italian sausage,
  casings removed and sausage crumbled
1½ tablespoons ground cumin
1½ tablespoons chili powder

1½ tablespoons cayenne pepper
1 tablespoon kosher salt
Black pepper to taste
3 Spanish onions, chopped
3 red bell peppers, chopped
4 garlic cloves, minced
2 jalapeño chiles, seeded if desired
  and chopped
1 (28-ounce) can crushed tomatoes
4 cups beef broth

Sauté the bacon in a large stockpot or Dutch oven until rendered. Toss the beef chuck, pork and sausage with the cumin, chili powder, cayenne pepper, salt and black pepper in a bowl. Add to the bacon and cook over medium-high heat until the meats are brown, stirring frequently; drain. (Brown the meat in batches, if desired.) Stir in the onions, bell peppers, garlic and chiles. Reduce the heat and cook for 15 minutes or until the vegetables are tender, stirring occasionally.

Stir the tomatoes and 1 cup of the broth into the beef mixture and reduce the heat to a simmer. Simmer for a minimum of 6 hours, adding the remaining broth 1 cup at a time as needed to prevent the chili from becoming too dry, stirring occasionally. Ladle into chili bowls. The longer the chili simmers, the more tender the meat mixture and the tastier the chili. See anecdote for garnish ideas.

*Serves 12*

*MY HUSBAND'S FRIEND HAS AN ANNUAL CHILI PARTY THE FRIDAY AFTER THANKSGIVING AND SERVES THIS AMAZING CONCOCTION. IT IS CHUNKY, STEW-LIKE, AND DELICIOUS! I'VE OMITTED THE BEANS, WHICH MAKES IT EVEN HEARTIER THAN THE ORIGINAL. THIS IS BEST MADE THE DAY BEFORE AND ALLOWED TO SIMMER FOREVER ON THE STOVETOP. REHEAT AND SERVE WITH WHATEVER CHILI SIDES YOU ENJOY: CHEESE, CHOPPED RAW ONION, OR SOUR CREAM. GO FOR IT!*

# TURKEY CHILI

*4 flour tortillas, cut into strips*  
*1 large onion, chopped*  
*2 garlic cloves, minced*  
*1 cup olive oil*  
*1 pound ground turkey*  
*1 tablespoon dried oregano*  
*1 tablespoon ground cumin*  
*2 teaspoons coriander*  
*Salt and pepper to taste*

*2 cups chicken broth*  
*1 (16-ounce) can kidney beans, drained*  
*1 (16-ounce) can black beans, drained*  
*1 (15-ounce) can lentils, drained*  
*1 (15-ounce) can diced tomatoes*  
*1 ancho chile, seeded and finely chopped*  
*1 jalapeño chile, seeded and finely chopped*  
*Shredded Monterey Jack cheese*  
*Chopped cilantro*

Arrange the tortilla strips in a single layer on a baking sheet. Toast at 375 degrees until crisp. Remove to a platter to cool.

Sauté the onion and garlic in the olive oil in a stockpot until the onion is tender. Add the turkey and cook until brown and crumbly, stirring frequently. Stir in the oregano, cumin, coriander, salt and pepper.

Cook for 5 minutes. Add the broth, beans, lentils, tomatoes, ancho chile and jalapeño chile and mix well. Cook, partially covered, for 40 to 50 minutes or until thickened, stirring occasionally. Ladle into chili bowls and top with cheese, cilantro and toasted tortilla strips.

*Serves 6 to 8*

*THIS IS A FRESH AND LIGHT ALTERNATIVE TO THE TRADITIONAL RED CHILI. THE ADDITION OF LENTILS LENDS A NUTTY AND WARM FLAVOR TO A FAMILY FAVORITE.*

# IRISH STEW

*1 pound small Yukon Gold potatoes, peeled and cut into 1-inch rounds*

*2 onions, cut into halves and thinly sliced*

*2 pounds lamb shoulder, cut into 1-inch pieces*

*1 teaspoon coarse salt*

*Freshly ground pepper to taste*

*2 teaspoons coarsely chopped fresh thyme*

*3 cups chicken stock*

*1 cup water*

*2 pounds small whole Yukon Gold potatoes, peeled*

*1 teaspoon coarse salt*

*2 tablespoons finely chopped fresh flat-leaf parsley*

Arrange the potato rounds over the bottom of a 5- or 6-quart Dutch oven. Layer with one of the onions, the lamb, 1 teaspoon salt, pepper, thyme and the remaining onion. Pour the stock and water over the prepared layers. Top with 2 pounds whole potatoes, 1 teaspoon salt and pepper.

Cover and bring to a boil over medium-high heat. Bake at 325 degrees for 2 hours; do not stir. Sprinkle with the parsley and serve.

*Serves 4 to 6*

*MY HUSBAND IS IRISH, BUT COULD NEVER BRING HIMSELF TO EAT CORNED BEEF AND CABBAGE ON ST. PATRICK'S DAY. AT OUR HOUSE, WE HAVE IRISH STEW PAIRED WITH GUINNESS! LET IT SIMMER.... A HEAVY POT WITH A TIGHT-FITTING LID WORKS BEST. DON'T LIFT THE LID OR STIR THE STEW; THE MORE HEAT AND MOISTURE THERE IS, THE MORE TENDER THE RESULTS WILL BE.*

# Marbledale Mains

# Tuckahoe, New York

*"Marbledale Mains"*

*Tuckahoe's Marbledale Avenue is named for the marble quarries of the past that made this village an important part of many famous architectural monuments.*

Located in the Town of Eastchester, the Village of Tuckahoe sits on .6 square miles of land and is bordered by the Village of Bronxville to its south and the City of Yonkers to the west. Like many place-names throughout Westchester County, "Tuckahoe" is derived from the Native American word meaning "place of tuckah." Tuckah is a mushroom-like plant used for food. Tuckahoe was incorporated as a village in 1903.

In 1822 high quality white marble was found in Tuckahoe, and the Tuckahoe marble quarries soon opened. The discovery of this marble led to the development of an industry that had a great effect on Tuckahoe's economic and social life. Due to its location, which is less than twenty miles from New York City and only five miles from navigable waters, Tuckahoe became a major producer of marble for some of America's most enduring architectural masterpieces, including St. Patrick's Cathedral, the Washington Monument, and the U.S. Capitol, as well as other projects throughout the world.

The Junior League of Bronxville has long been a presence in Tuckahoe, from working with the elderly at the Tuckahoe Senior Center and assisting them through Senior Citizens Coordinating Council and the Senior Personnel Agency, to operating the Pennypincher thrift shop. Among its many other efforts, The JLB has also aided in the development of the Jansen Memorial Hospice and the Treehouse Program at Bereavement Center of Westchester, which offers grief support to children suffering the loss of a parent or sibling.

PHOTO: PARKWAY BRIDLE PATH

## Marbledale Mains
# Entrées

Roasted Prime Rib

Grilled Flank Steak with Rosemary

Cheeseburger Meat Loaf

Horseradish Mashed Potato Shepherd's Pie

Everyone's Favorite Pork Tenderloin

Pork Chops with Cranberry, Port and Rosemary Sauce

Moose's Ribs, Best Ribs Ever!

Veal Cutlet alla Milanese

Artichoke Chicken

Chicken Marbella

Chicken, Sausage and Leek Pie

Spicy and Garlicky Cashew Chicken

Mussels in White Wine

Sautéed Scallops and Sweet Pea Risotto

Parmesan Scallops

Shrimp with Feta Cheese

Shrimp and Pancetta Pappardelle

Stir-Fry Singapore Shrimp Curry

Sesame Noodles

Orecchiette with Wild Mushroom cream

Lasagna

Linguini with Squash, Bacon and Goat Cheese

Creamy Macaroni and Cheese

# ROASTED PRIME RIB

1 prime rib roast
3 tablespoons all-purpose flour
1 tablespoon dry mustard
2 teaspoons salt
2 teaspoons freshly ground pepper
1 cup dry red wine

Request the butcher to debone the roast, reserving the short ribs for this recipe. Mix the flour, dry mustard, salt and pepper in a bowl. Rub over the surface of the roast.

Tie the short ribs with kitchen twine and arrange in a large roasting pan. Place the roast fat side up on top of the ribs. Place the roasting pan on an oven rack in the lower third of the oven.

Roast at 450 degrees for 20 minutes. Reduce the oven temperature to 325 degrees. Roast for about 15 minutes per pound or until a meat thermometer registers 145 degrees for medium-rare, basting frequently with the pan juices and pouring the wine over the roast after 1¾ hours.

Remove the roast and ribs to a platter and let stand for 30 minutes. Slice the roast and serve with the ribs and horseradish sauce.

*Serves 10*

MAKE SURE THAT YOU HAVE THE BUTCHER DEBONE THE ROAST—SAVING THE RIBS FOR THIS RECIPE—AND GET THE BEST QUALITY MEAT POSSIBLE. IT REALLY DOES MAKE A DIFFERENCE IN HOW THIS SHOW-STOPPER ROAST TURNS OUT!

# GRILLED FLANK STEAK WITH ROSEMARY

*½ cup soy sauce*
*½ cup olive oil*
*4½ tablespoons honey*
*6 large garlic cloves*
*3 tablespoons chopped fresh rosemary, or*
   *1 tablespoon dried rosemary*
*1½ teaspoons salt*
*Pepper to taste*
*1 (2¼-pound) flank steak*

Mix the soy sauce, olive oil, honey, garlic, rosemary, salt and pepper in a 9×13-inch dish. Add the steak and turn to coat. Marinate, covered, in the refrigerator for 2 hours, turning occasionally; drain.

Grill or broil the steak for 4 minutes per side for medium-rare or to the desired degree of doneness. Remove the steak to a hard work surface and let stand for 5 minutes. Cut across the grain into thin strips. Arrange the steak on a serving platter and serve immediately.

*Serves 6*

*The first year that my husband and I were married, we took turns having dinner parties with our close friends—a fun way to test recipes and practice hosting. Our friends served this, and fourteen years later it is still a delectable tried-and-true dish that we turn to over and over again.*

# Cheeseburger Meat Loaf

1 carrot, chopped
1 yellow onion, chopped
⅔ cup milk
3 slices dry bread, torn
2 eggs
2 teaspoons salt
2 teaspoons pepper
2 pounds chopped beef, pork and veal mixture
1 cup (4 ounces) shredded Cheddar cheese
½ cup packed light brown sugar
½ cup ketchup
2 tablespoons Dijon mustard

Process the carrot, onion, milk, bread, eggs, salt and pepper in a food processor for 1 minute and pour into a bowl. Add the chopped beef mixture and cheese and mix until combined.

Shape into a loaf in a loaf pan. Mix the brown sugar, ketchup and Dijon mustard in a bowl and pour over the meat loaf. Place the loaf pan on a baking sheet to catch any drippings and arrange on the oven rack. Bake at 350 degrees for 1½ hours. Let stand for 10 minutes before serving.

*Serves 8*

*I was never a meat loaf fan until my best friend shared with me this satisfying recipe. It tastes like a mashed-up, moist cheeseburger. Serve with buttery potatoes—yum!*

# HORSERADISH MASHED POTATO SHEPHERD'S PIE

7 or 8 large Yukon Gold potatoes, peeled
  and cut into chunks

Kosher salt to taste

½ cup milk

3 to 4 tablespoons prepared horseradish

Freshly ground pepper to taste

2 tablespoons olive oil

3 parsnips, peeled and chopped

2 carrots, peeled and chopped

1 large Spanish onion, chopped

1 bay leaf

2 pounds ground lamb or beef

3 tablespoons all-purpose flour

1½ cups beef broth

1 tablespoon Worcestershire sauce

2 to 3 tablespoons chopped fresh chives

Combine the potatoes with enough cold salted water to generously cover in a stockpot and bring to a boil. Reduce the heat and simmer for 15 minutes or until the potatoes are tender; drain. Mash the potatoes in a bowl, adding the milk during the mashing process. Stir in the horseradish and season with salt and pepper.

Heat the olive oil in a large deep skillet over medium heat. Add the parsnips, carrots, onion, bay leaf, salt and pepper. Cook for 8 to 10 minutes or until the vegetables are tender, stirring frequently. Crumble the lamb into the skillet and cook for 5 minutes, stirring frequently; drain, if desired. Sprinkle the flour over the lamb mixture and cook for 1 minute. Stir in the broth. Cook for 1 to 2 minutes or until thickened, stirring constantly. Add the Worcestershire sauce, salt and pepper and mix well. Discard the bay leaf.

Spoon the lamb mixture into a greased shallow medium baking dish and top with the mashed potatoes, spreading to the edge. Bake at 450 degrees for 5 to 10 minutes or until golden brown. Sprinkle with the chives.

Serves 4 to 6

THIS IS A HEARTY AND SATISFYING DISH TO MAKE EARLIER IN THE DAY AND JUST THROW IN THE OVEN TO WARM FOR A COZY DINNER. I SOMETIMES TOP THE MASHED POTATOES WITH MY FAVORITE CHEESE FOR AN EXTRA TREAT!

# EVERYONE'S FAVORITE PORK TENDERLOIN

2½ pounds pork tenderloin
⅔ cup grainy Dijon mustard
¾ cup packed brown sugar
2 teaspoons Worcestershire sauce

Trim any fat from the pork and score with a fork, making long grooves. Coat the pork with the Dijon mustard and pat the brown sugar over the surface.

Arrange in a roasting pan or baking pan sprayed with nonstick cooking spray. Drizzle the Worcestershire sauce over the top. Bake at 350 degrees for 30 minutes. Check for doneness. Let stand for several minutes before slicing.

*Serves 4 to 6*

MY SISTER-IN-LAW SERVED THIS TO A GUY SHE HAD A HUGE CRUSH ON. IT MUST HAVE WORKED BECAUSE THEY ARE NOW MARRIED. THEY DO SAY THE WAY TO A MAN'S HEART IS THROUGH HIS STOMACH!

# PORK CHOPS WITH CRANBERRY, PORT AND ROSEMARY SAUCE

*4 (1-inch-thick) pork rib chops*
*Kosher salt and freshly ground pepper to taste*
*1 teaspoon minced fresh rosemary*
*2 tablespoons unsalted butter, softened*
*¾ cup chicken broth*
*¾ cup tawny port*
*1¾ teaspoons minced fresh rosemary*
*1 cup whole cranberry sauce*

Season the pork chops with salt and pepper and sprinkle with 1 teaspoon rosemary. Melt the butter in a large heavy skillet until the butter begins to brown. Add the pork chops and cook for about 5 minutes per side or until brown and cooked through. Remove the pork chops to a platter and cover to keep warm, reserving the pan drippings.

Stir the broth, wine and 1¾ teaspoons rosemary into the reserved pan drippings. Cook over high heat for 4 minutes or until slightly reduced, stirring frequently. Add the cranberry sauce and bring to a boil. Reduce the heat to medium and simmer for 7 minutes or until the sauce is thickened. Season with salt and pepper. Spoon the sauce over the pork chops. Serve immediately.

*Serves 4*

THE DAY AFTER THANKSGIVING THIS DISH IS A WELCOME CHANGE FROM THE TRADITIONAL FARE WE HAVE ALL ENJOYED. IT IS A SATISFYING WAY TO MAKE USE OF EXTRA CRANBERRY SAUCE, AND YOU DON'T HAVE TO EAT TURKEY YET AGAIN!

# MOOSE'S RIBS, BEST RIBS EVER!

2 (12-ounce) bottles beer
2 (12-ounce) cans cola
2 cups sliced onions
½ cup soy sauce
½ cup salt
¼ cup sugar
2 tablespoons hot red pepper sauce
2 tablespoons liquid smoke
1 tablespoon freshly ground pepper
6 garlic cloves, crushed

10 bay leaves
1 rack baby back ribs
¾ cup ketchup
¼ cup chili sauce
3 tablespoons molasses
2 tablespoons orange juice
1 tablespoon Worcestershire sauce
1 tablespoon liquid smoke
1 tablespoon chili powder
½ small onion, chopped

Combine the beer and cola in a stockpot large enough to hold the ribs. Stir in the sliced onions, soy sauce, salt, sugar, hot sauce, 2 tablespoons liquid smoke, the pepper, garlic and bay leaves. Simmer over medium heat for 10 minutes and add the ribs. If the ribs are not completely immersed in the liquid add enough water to cover. Simmer for 3 hours or until the meat is just about ready to fall off the bones, checking every 10 minutes.

Mix the ketchup, chili sauce, molasses, orange juice, Worcestershire sauce, 1 tablespoon liquid smoke, the chili powder and chopped onion in a saucepan. Simmer for 20 minutes or until of a sauce consistency, stirring occasionally.

Brush the ribs with the sauce and arrange on the grill rack. Grill over medium heat for a few minutes or just until glazed, turning occasionally. Serve the remaining sauce with the ribs for dipping.

*Serves 8 to 10*

*THIS IS A FLAVORSOME AND UNCOMPLICATED RECIPE. DON'T WORRY ABOUT COOKING THE RIBS TOO LONG. YOU CAN'T REALLY OVERCOOK THEM UNLESS YOU REALLY, REALLY TRY!*

# Veal Cutlets alla Milanese

Dry rustic bread

4 cups baby arugula

Good-quality olive oil to taste

Salt to taste

Juice of 1 lemon

½ cup (2 ounces) grated Parmigiano-
    Reggiano cheese or grana padano cheese

1 garlic clove, minced

2 tablespoons chopped flat-leaf parsley

1 cup all-purpose flour

1 teaspoon salt

Freshly ground pepper to taste

2 eggs

2 tablespoons water

4 thinly sliced veal scallopini

½ cup canola oil

½ cup olive oil

2 or 3 vine-ripened tomatoes,
    seeded and chopped

Process enough bread slices with crusts in a food processor to measure 2 cups. Toss the arugula with olive oil to taste in a bowl. Season generously with salt to taste. Add the lemon juice and toss again.

Combine the bread crumbs, cheese, garlic and parsley in a shallow dish and mix well. Mix the flour, 1 teaspoon salt and pepper in a shallow dish. Whisk the eggs and water in a bowl until blended. Pound the veal ⅛ inch thick between sheets of waxed paper using a meat mallet. Coat the veal lightly with the flour mixture, dip in the egg mixture and then coat with the bread crumb mixture.

Heat the canola oil and ½ cup olive oil in a skillet. Add the cutlets and cook until brown on both sides. Drain on paper towels. Arrange one cutlet on each of four serving plates and top each equally with the dressed arugula and chopped tomatoes. Garnish with lemon wedges and serve immediately.

*Serves 4*

*My mother's veal cutlets were my favorite dish growing up. As they were cooking, their irresistible aroma would immediately draw me into the kitchen. Served with this simple arugula and tomato salad—as they are served in many northern Italian restaurants—they make a lovely presentation and a very satisfying main course.*

# ARTICHOKE CHICKEN

*All-purpose flour*
*Dried tarragon*
*Salt and pepper to taste*
*1 whole chicken, cut into 8 pieces*
*Olive oil*
*1 cup chicken stock*
*½ cup white wine*
*Juice of 1 lemon*
*2 (14-ounce) cans artichoke hearts, drained and*
  *cut into halves*
*Sprigs of parsley*
*Thinly sliced lemon rounds*
*Hot cooked rice or noodles*

Mix flour, tarragon, salt and pepper in a shallow dish. Coat the chicken with the flour mixture. Brown the chicken lightly on all sides in olive oil in a sauté pan; drain. Add the stock and wine to the sauté pan and simmer for 5 minutes.

Remove the chicken and pan juices to a baking pan and drizzle with the lemon juice. Scatter the artichokes around the chicken and top with parsley and lemon rounds.

Bake at 350 degrees for 1 hour or until the chicken is cooked through. Serve over hot cooked rice or noodles. Add wine and broth to the pan drippings to make gravy, if desired.

*Serves 4 to 6*

*MY MOTHER-IN-LAW MADE SURE THAT I RECEIVED MY HUSBAND'S FAVORITE RECIPES WHEN WE GOT MARRIED. I CANNOT ARGUE WHEN IT COMES TO THIS DISH—IT IS ONE OF MY HUSBAND'S FAVORITES AND NOW ONE OF MINE, TOO!*

# CHICKEN MARBELLA

*2 chickens, each cut into 4 or 8 pieces*
*1½ cups white wine*
*1 cup olive oil*
*1 cup packed brown sugar*
*¾ cup red wine vinegar*
*2 cups pitted prunes*
*1 cup pitted green olives*
*1 garlic bulb, separated into cloves and chopped*
*⅓ cup capers*
*¼ cup oregano*
*6 bay leaves*
*Salt and pepper to taste*
*¼ cup fresh parsley, chopped*

Place each cut-up chicken in a large sealable plastic bag. Whisk the wine, olive oil, brown sugar and vinegar in a bowl until the brown sugar dissolves. Stir in the prunes, olives, garlic, capers, oregano, bay leaves, salt and pepper. Pour equal portions of the marinade over each chicken and seal tightly. Turn to coat.

Marinate in the refrigerator for 8 to 10 hours, turning occasionally. Drain, reserving the marinade. Arrange the chicken in a single layer in a baking dish and pour the reserved marinade over the top. Bake at 350 degrees for 1 hour, basting frequently with the marinade. Discard the bay leaves and sprinkle with the parsley. Serve with hot cooked white rice.

*Serves 6 to 8*

*I MAY BE SWEDISH, BUT THIS MEDITERRANEAN DISH IS MY FAVORITE MEAL TO SERVE AT DINNER PARTIES. I LOVE THAT IT CAN BE PREPARED A DAY AHEAD IN A ZIPLOCK BAG UNTIL READY TO BAKE. ALSO, IT TASTES EVEN MORE ROBUST AND DELICIOUS THE NEXT DAY FOR LEFTOVERS.*

# CHICKEN, SAUSAGE AND LEEK PIE

½ (17-ounce) package puff pastry
1 tablespoon olive oil
1 tablespoon unsalted butter
3 leeks, trimmed and sliced
3 carrots, peeled and sliced
2 ribs celery, sliced
Pinch of dried thyme
2 pounds boneless skinless chicken thighs,
    cut into 2-inch pieces

1½ tablespoons all-purpose flour
1 cup white wine
1 cup milk
Salt and pepper to taste
10 ounces sweet pork sausage,
    casings removed
Olive oil for browning
1 handful of fresh parsley, chopped
1 egg, beaten

Thaw the puff pastry using the package directions. Heat 1 tablespoon olive oil and the butter in a heavy saucepan or Dutch oven over medium heat. Add the leeks, carrots, celery and thyme and cook until the vegetables are golden brown. Stir in the chicken and reduce the heat to low.

Cook for 10 minutes. Increase the heat and mix in the flour until combined. Stir in the wine, milk, salt and pepper. Decrease the heat and simmer for 35 minutes or until the chicken is tender and the sauce is thickened, stirring occasionally.

Shape the sausage into small balls. Brown the sausage balls in olive oil in a sauté pan; drain. Pour the chicken mixture into a deep-dish pie plate and sprinkle with the sausage balls and parsley.

Unroll the pastry and arrange over the top of the chicken mixture. Pinch the pastry over the edge and trim. Brush the pastry with the egg. Make crisscross slits in the pastry to vent. Bake at 425 degrees for 40 minutes or until golden brown.

*Serves 6*

CHICKEN POTPIES CAN MAKE YOU SNORE, BUT THE COMBINATION OF HEARTY LEEKS AND A SCATTERING OF MOIST PORK MEATBALLS ELEVATES THIS TO A DISH YOU CAN BE PROUD TO SERVE YOUR GUESTS.

# SPICY AND GARLICKY CASHEW CHICKEN

*1 cup salted roasted cashews*
*¼ cup canola oil or safflower oil*
*4 garlic cloves, coarsely chopped*
*2 tablespoons chopped cilantro*
*2 tablespoons soy sauce*
*2 tablespoons water*
*2 teaspoons brown sugar*

*1 or 2 jalapeño chiles, seeded*
*    if desired and sliced*
*Juice of 1 lime*
*Kosher salt and freshly ground pepper*
*    to taste*
*3 pounds chicken thighs and/or legs*
*¼ cup chopped cilantro*

Combine the cashews, canola oil, garlic, 2 tablespoons cilantro, the soy sauce, water, brown sugar, chiles and lime juice in a blender or food processor. Process until smooth, scraping the side as necessary. Taste and season with salt and pepper.

Season the chicken with salt and pepper. Coat the chicken with some of the cashew mixture, reserving the remainder. Marinate at room temperature while you preheat the grill or broiler. Or, marinate in sealable plastic bags in the refrigerator for up to 12 hours, turning occasionally.

Grill or broil for 20 to 30 minutes or until the chicken is crisp, golden brown and cooked through, turning frequently. Remove to a serving platter and sprinkle with ¼ cup cilantro. Serve with the remaining cashew mixture and lime wedges.

*Serves 4 to 6*

*THIS IS A GREAT DISH TO MAKE WHEN HEADED OUT OF TOWN FOR THE WEEKEND AND YOU NEED TO BRING A PARTLY PREPARED DISH. THE CHICKEN CAN MARINATE IN ZIPLOCK BAGS IN A COOLER WHILE YOU TRAVEL, AND WHEN YOU ARRIVE AT YOUR DESTINATION, IT'S READY TO THROW ON THE GRILL AND FEED HUNGRY TRAVELERS! BOTH CHILDREN AND ADULTS LOVE THE NUTTY FLAVORS!*

# MUSSELS IN WHITE WINE

*4 pounds fresh live mussels*
*¼ cup (½ stick) unsalted butter*
*2 shallots, chopped*
*2 cups chardonnay or pinot grigio*
*¼ cup fresh thyme*
*¼ cup fresh parsley*
*1 tablespoon chopped fresh basil*
*1 or 2 bay leaves*
*Salt and pepper to taste*

Scrub and clean the mussels under running water, discarding the beards. The mussels should have tightly closed shells with no cracks. Any mussels that are open and do not close when lightly squeezed should be discarded.

Melt the butter in a Dutch oven over low heat. Add the shallots and cook until tender. Stir in the wine, thyme, parsley, basil, bay leaf, salt and pepper. Increase the heat to medium and cook for 2 minutes. Stir in the mussels.

Cook, covered, for about 7 minutes, discarding any mussels that do not open. Discard the bay leaves. Serve from the Dutch oven with a bottle of chardonnay or pinot grigio and a baguette of crusty French bread.

*Serves 4*

*THIS RECIPE WAS SUBMITTED WITH A DEAR FRIEND OF MINE IN MIND. THE LAST TIME I MADE THIS DISH AT A DINNER PARTY, SHE WAS FOUND HOVERING OVER THE STOVE, SPOON IN HAND, MAKING SURE THERE WERE NO LEFTOVERS!*

# Sautéed Scallops and Sweet Pea Risotto

1 cup fresh or thawed frozen sweet baby peas

6½ cups chicken stock

1 tablespoon olive oil

3 shallots, minced

2 garlic cloves, minced

14 ounces arborio rice

1 cup dry vermouth

1 cup fresh or thawed frozen sweet baby peas

¼ cup (½ stick) unsalted butter

½ cup (2 ounces) grated fresh
    Parmesan cheese

1 tablespoon olive oil

1 tablespoon butter

1 pound jumbo scallops

Kosher salt and pepper to taste

1 tablespoon olive oil

Process 1 cup peas and ½ cup of the stock in a blender until puréed. Heat the remaining 6 cups stock in a saucepan. Keep warm over low heat. Heat 1 tablespoon olive oil in a saucepan and add the shallots and garlic. Cook for 2 to 3 minutes or until the shallots are tender, stirring constantly. Add the rice and stir until combined. Decrease the heat and mix in the vermouth, stirring constantly.

Cook until the liquid is absorbed, stirring constantly. Add the warm stock 1 cup at a time, cooking until the stock is absorbed after each addition and stirring constantly. The mixture will be creamy at the end of the process. Fold in the pea purée and 1 cup whole peas. Remove from the heat and stir in ¼ cup butter and the cheese. Let stand, covered.

Heat 1 tablespoon olive oil and 1 tablespoon butter in a sauté pan until the butter melts. Pat the scallops dry with paper towels and season with salt and pepper. Add to the olive oil mixture and sauté for 5 to 8 minutes or until golden brown on both sides. Spoon equal portions of the risotto onto serving plates and top each serving with several of the scallops. Drizzle with 1 tablespoon olive oil and serve immediately.

*Serves 4 to 6*

*THERE IS NOTHING BETTER THAN A PERFECTLY COOKED SCALLOP—SEARED AND GOLDEN ON THE OUTSIDE BUT PERFECTLY JUST HEATED THROUGH ON THE INSIDE. THE COLOR OF THIS RISOTTO IS SUCH A PRETTY SHADE OF GREEN AND MAKES A GREAT NEST FOR THE SCALLOPS.*

# Parmesan Scallops

*½ to ¾ cup bread crumbs*
*1 pound sea scallops*
*2 tablespoons vegetable oil*
*3 to 4 ounces Parmesan cheese, shredded*
*1 or 2 lemons, cut into wedges*

Place the bread crumbs in a sealable plastic bag and add the scallops in batches; seal tightly. Toss to coat lightly. Heat the oil in an ovenproof skillet until hot and then mix in the scallops.

Broil for 3 to 4 minutes or until the scallops are opaque and slightly firm. Sprinkle with the cheese and broil for 45 to 60 seconds or until golden brown; watch carefully. Serve with lemon wedges.

*Serves 4*

*THIS RECIPE COMES FROM MY EX-HUSBAND. BAD HUSBAND, GREAT COOK!*

# SHRIMP WITH FETA CHEESE

*¼ cup olive oil*
*1 large onion, chopped*
*4 garlic cloves, chopped*
*1 tablespoon fresh oregano, minced, or more to taste*
*1 tablespoon fresh parsley, minced, or more to taste*
*Freshly ground pepper to taste*
*1 (28-ounce) can crushed tomatoes*
*2¼ pounds large shrimp, peeled and deveined*
*¼ cup olive oil*
*¼ cup ouzo*
*1 pound good-quality feta cheese, crumbled*
*Hot cooked rice*

Heat ¼ cup olive oil in a small or medium skillet. Add the onion, garlic, 1 tablespoon oregano, 1 tablespoon parsley and pepper and sauté for about 15 minutes. Stir in the tomatoes and decrease the heat. Cook for 10 minutes, stirring occasionally.

Sauté the shrimp in ¼ cup olive oil in a large skillet for 1 minute or just until the shrimp begin to turn pink, adding oregano and parsley to taste. Remove from the heat and stir in the liqueur. Ignite with a long match and allow the flames to subside. Stir in the tomato mixture and the cheese. Cook for 3 to 4 minutes or until heated through, stirring frequently. Serve over hot cooked rice.

*Serves 4*

*EVERY TIME THAT I PREPARE THIS DISH—BETWEEN THE SMELLS OF OUZO, SHRIMP, AND FETA—I AM TRANSPORTED BACK TO MYKONOS!*

# SHRIMP AND PANCETTA PAPPARDELLE

*16 ounces dried or fresh pappardelle*
*Salt to taste*
*¼ cup olive oil*
*6 ounces pancetta, chopped*
*1 red onion, finely sliced*
*3 garlic cloves, minced*
*½ cup white wine*
*2 tablespoons fresh lemon juice*
*1 teaspoon kosher salt*
*½ teaspoon crushed red pepper flakes*
*2 pounds large shrimp, peeled, deveined and butterflied*
*½ cup fresh parsley, chopped*

Cook the pasta in boiling salted water in a stockpot using the package directions until al dente. Drain, reserving ½ cup of the cooking liquid. Cover to keep warm.

Heat the olive oil in a large sauté pan over medium heat. Add the pancetta and cook for 5 to 6 minutes or until light brown, stirring frequently. Add the onion and sauté for about 2 minutes. Stir in the garlic and cook for 30 seconds, being careful not to burn the garlic. Stir in the wine, lemon juice, 1 teaspoon salt and the red pepper flakes. Mix in the shrimp.

Cook for 5 minutes or until the shrimp turn pink. Add the pasta to the shrimp mixture and mix well. Cook for 1 minute, adding the reserved cooking liquid if needed to create more sauce. Sprinkle with the parsley. Serve with grated Parmesan cheese.

*Serves 4 to 6*

*THIS IS THE PASTA DISH I MAKE WHEN I HAVE A "GIRLS ONLY" DINNER OR LUNCH, BECAUSE EVERYTHING IN IT IS A PRETTY SHADE OF PINK—THE RED ONION, SHRIMP, PANCETTA, AND RED PEPPER FLAKES!*

# STIR-FRY SINGAPORE SHRIMP CURRY

¼ cup dry sherry

2 teaspoons cornstarch

¼ cup soy sauce

¼ cup canned unsweetened coconut milk

2 tablespoons molasses

4 teaspoons curry powder

2 teaspoons chili garlic sauce

¼ cup finely chopped fresh ginger

3 garlic cloves, minced

4 scallions, cut into 1-inch pieces

3 jalapeño chiles, seeded and chopped

¼ cup vegetable oil

3 cups thinly sliced napa cabbage

2 red bell peppers, cut into thin strips

1 pound jumbo shrimp, peeled and deveined

6 tablespoons fresh cilantro, chopped

Hot cooked jasmine rice

Mix the sherry and cornstarch in a bowl until blended. Stir in the soy sauce, coconut milk, molasses, curry powder and chili garlic sauce.

Stir-fry the ginger, garlic, scallions and chiles in the oil in a large nonstick skillet over high heat for 1 minute. Add the cabbage and bell peppers and stir-fry for about 2 minutes. Stir in the sherry mixture and simmer for 2 minutes or until thickened, stirring frequently. Add the shrimp and stir-fry over medium-high heat until the shrimp turn pink. Stir in 3 tablespoons of the cilantro.

Spoon the shrimp mixture over hot cooked jasmine rice on a serving platter. Sprinkle with the remaining 3 tablespoons cilantro. Garnish with lime wedges.

*Serves 6 to 8*

*Since moving from Manhattan, we miss the plethora of ethnic goodies available at any time of the day or night. This recipe is on par with some of the best Thai food that I have ever had.*

# Sesame Noodles

*32 ounces angel hair pasta*
*Salt to taste*
*1 bunch broccoli, cut into florets*
*1 tablespoon Chinese sesame oil*
*1 pound mushrooms, sliced*
*½ cup soy sauce*
*½ cup Chinese sesame oil*
*3 tablespoons wine vinegar*
*3 tablespoons sugar*
*2 tablespoons hot pepper oil*
*2 tablespoons oyster sauce*
*1 tablespoon salt*
*1 bunch scallions, trimmed and chopped*

Cook the pasta in boiling salted water in a stockpot using the package directions until al dente; drain. Blanch the broccoli in boiling water in a saucepan for 3 to 4 minutes. Drain and plunge the broccoli immediately into an ice bath to stop the cooking process and maintain the bright green color; drain again. Heat 1 tablespoon sesame oil in a sauté pan and add the mushrooms. Sauté for 3 to 5 minutes.

Whisk the soy sauce, ½ cup sesame oil, the vinegar, sugar, hot pepper oil, oyster sauce and 1 tablespoon salt in a bowl until emulsified. Toss with the pasta in a large bowl to coat. Mix in the broccoli and mushrooms and sprinkle with the scallions. Serve at room temperature.

*Serves 10 to 12*

*I OFTEN MAKE THIS DISH WHEN WE ARE HEADED OUT OF TOWN FOR THE WEEKEND WITH FAMILY AND FRIENDS. IT MAKES A TON AND THE NOODLES ARE EVEN BETTER AFTER THEY HAVE BEEN MADE AND SIT OVERNIGHT. KIDS LOVE THE PEANUTTY FLAVOR!*

# ORECCHIETTE WITH WILD MUSHROOM CREAM

*16 ounces orecchiette*

*Kosher salt to taste*

*2 tablespoons olive oil*

*2 pounds shallots, finely chopped*

*2 garlic cloves, minced*

*1 quart assorted fresh wild mushrooms
    (chanterelles, shiitake, cremini, porcini
    and/or oyster), trimmed and sliced*

*1 cup beef broth*

*1 cup heavy cream*

*Pepper to taste*

*2 tablespoons chopped fresh chives*

*Grated Parmesan cheese to taste*

Cook the pasta in boiling salted water in a stockpot using the package directions until al dente; drain. Heat the olive oil in a large sauté pan over high heat and add the shallots and garlic.

Sauté for about 1 minute or until the shallots are tender; do not allow the garlic to burn. Stir in the mushrooms and sauté for about 5 minutes or until the mushrooms are tender and juicy. Add the broth and mix well.

Cook for 5 minutes or until the liquid is reduced, stirring frequently. Stir in the cream and cook until thickened. Season with salt and pepper.

Combine the pasta with the mushroom mixture in a serving bowl and mix well. Sprinkle with the chives and cheese. Serve immediately.

*Serves 4 to 6*

*WHENEVER I MAKE ORECCHIETTE-SHAPED PASTAS, IT ALWAYS REMINDS ME OF A HAPPY SMILEY FACE! IT'S A GREAT MEAT SUBSTITUTE, ESPECIALLY WHEN YOU GET A GOOD MIX OF EARTHY, SEASONAL MUSHROOMS.*

# LASAGNA

8 ounces 85% lean ground beef

8 ounces hot Italian sausage,
  casings removed

1 (16-ounce) can crushed tomatoes

1 (12-ounce) can tomato paste

2 garlic cloves, crushed or finely chopped

1 tablespoon fresh parsley, chopped

1 tablespoon fresh basil, chopped

1½ teaspoons salt

10 ounces lasagna noodles

Salt to taste

32 ounces ricotta cheese

½ cup (2 ounces) grated Parmesan cheese

2 eggs, beaten

2 tablespoons fresh parsley, chopped

½ teaspoon freshly ground pepper

1 pound mozzarella cheese, shredded or
  thinly sliced

Brown the ground beef and sausage in a large saucepan or Dutch oven, stirring until crumbly; drain. Stir in the tomatoes, tomato paste, garlic, 1 tablespoon parsley, the basil and 1½ teaspoons salt. Simmer for 45 minutes or until thickened, stirring occasionally.

Cook the pasta in boiling salted water in a stockpot using the package directions until al dente; drain. Rinse the pasta with cold water and drain again. Mix the ricotta cheese, Parmesan cheese, eggs, 2 tablespoons parsley and the pepper in a bowl.

Ladle a few tablespoons of the ground beef sauce into a 9×13-inch baking dish and spread over the bottom. Layer the noodles, ricotta cheese mixture, mozzarella cheese and remaining ground beef sauce in the prepared dish. Completely cover the last noodle layer with the ground beef sauce. Bake at 375 degrees for 30 minutes or until heated through. Let stand for 10 to 15 minutes before serving.

*Serves 8*

IN HIGH SCHOOL I WAS GIVEN THIS RECIPE TO BAKE FOR A TEACHERS' LUNCHEON. IT WAS THE BEST LASAGNA I HAD EVER TASTED. OVER THE YEARS, I HAVE PERFECTED IT.

# Linguini with Squash, Bacon and Goat Cheese

16 ounces linguini

8 ounces sliced bacon

1 (2- to 2½-pound) butternut squash, chopped (4 to 5 cups)

2 garlic cloves, minced

1½ cups chicken broth

1 teaspoon kosher salt

2 ounces goat cheese, crumbled

1 tablespoon olive oil

2 teaspoons freshly ground pepper

2 ounces goat cheese, crumbled

Cook the pasta in boiling water in a stockpot using the package directions; drain. Cover to keep warm.

Cook the bacon in a large skillet over medium heat for 5 minutes or until crisp. Remove the bacon to paper towels to drain, reserving 2 tablespoons of the bacon drippings in the skillet. Sauté the squash and garlic in the reserved bacon drippings over medium heat for 3 to 5 minutes. Stir in the broth and salt.

Simmer, covered, for 20 to 25 minutes or until the squash is cooked through and tender. Add 2 ounces cheese and mix until combined. Toss the squash mixture with the pasta in a large bowl until combined. Drizzle with the olive oil and top with the bacon, pepper and 2 ounces cheese. Serve immediately.

*Serves 4 to 6*

*My husband and I crave this dish when fall rolls around. Who says that you must eat chili when you watch football?*

# CREAMY MACARONI AND CHEESE

8 cups water
Salt to taste
16 ounces elbow macaroni
2 (12-ounce) cans evaporated 2% milk
1 cup chicken broth
3 tablespoons unsalted butter, cut
    into pieces

⅓ cup all-purpose flour
½ cup (2 ounces) grated fresh
    Parmesan cheese
1 tablespoon (scant) Dijon mustard
16 ounces shredded extra-sharp
    Cheddar cheese
Pepper to taste

Bring the water and salt to a boil in a stockpot and add the pasta. Cook using the package directions until al dente; drain. Spread the pasta on a large baking sheet to cool. Mix the evaporated milk and broth in a microwave-safe bowl and microwave for 3 minutes or until steamy.

Melt the butter in a Dutch oven over medium-high heat and whisk in the flour until combined. Add the hot milk mixture all at once and cook for 3 to 4 minutes or until thickened and bubbly, whisking constantly. Whisk in the Parmesan cheese and Dijon mustard. Remove from the heat and whisk in three-fourths of the Cheddar cheese. Mix in the pasta and season with salt and pepper.

Spoon into a 9×13-inch baking pan and sprinkle with the remaining Cheddar cheese. Bake at 350 degrees for 20 minutes or until heated through and bubbly.

*Serves 6 to 8*

AFTER I HAD CHILDREN I BEGAN LOOKING FOR THE BEST MACARONI AND CHEESE RECIPE THAT I COULD FIND. I TESTED AND WORKED ON ABOUT TWENTY RECIPES BEFORE I LANDED ON THIS ONE, AND I HAVE BEEN MAKING IT EVER SINCE.

# CEDAR KNOLLS COMPLEMENTS

# Yonkers, New York

*"Cedar Knolls Complements"*

*Cedar Knolls, one of the many historic areas dotting the City of Yonkers, New York, is a well-preserved enclave of historic homes dating from the turn of the last century.*

Yonkers, called the "Queen City of the Hudson," is the fourth-largest city in the state of New York and the largest city in Westchester County. The city's name comes from the term "Jonkheer," a Dutch word meaning young gentleman or nobleman, after its founder Adriaen Van der Donck. Founded in 1646 and the first city to be incorporated in Westchester County in 1872, Yonkers was a small farming town with an active waterfront that later grew through developing industry. After World War II, Yonkers became primarily a commuter city due to its excellent transportation infrastructure that includes two commuter railroad lines and five parkways and freeways, making it a fifteen-minute drive to Manhattan.

Spanning 20.3 square miles, Yonkers spreads from the Hudson River on the west to the Bronx River on the east, which separates it from Mount Vernon, Bronxville, Tuckahoe, and Eastchester, to the New York City borough of the Bronx to the south. Yonkers is home to the first golf course in the United States, the first FM radio broadcast, and the inventions of the first elevated train and safety elevator.

The Junior League of Bronxville's contributions to social services in Yonkers reach back to 1953 with The Children's Workshop, a music therapy program for children with cerebral palsy, which later grew into the Volunteer Educational Enrichment Program (VEEP), enhancing the lives of even more children in Yonkers. In the 1970s, The JLB funded, managed, and staffed a court assistance program for abused women, and more recently, The JLB was instrumental in supporting the Sharing Community Soup Kitchen and Greyston Family Inn and Music and Movement Program.

PHOTO: SNOW-COVERED BRIDGE

# CEDAR KNOLLS COMPLEMENTS
## VEGETABLES, SIDE DISHES AND SALADS

GRILLED ASPARAGUS

CARROT SOUFFLÉ

MAMAGIRL'S CORN PUDDING

PEAS WITH PROSCIUTTO

GRATIN POTATOES WITH LEEKS AND PORCINI MUSHROOMS

TWICE-BAKED POTATOES

SAUTÉED SPINACH WITH GARLIC AND GOLDEN RAISINS

MAPLE SWEET POTATOES

ZUCCHINI GENOVESE

QUICK RISOTTO

❧❧

CITRUS, RADICCHIO AND ENDIVE SALAD

CRUNCHY COCONUT AND WATERCRESS SALAD

DEEP-DISH LAYERED SALAD

MINTED CHICKEN AND CABBAGE SALAD

SHRIMP AND WHITE BEAN SALAD

SEAFOOD PASTA WITH LEMON SAFFRON HERB DRESSING

PASTA PRONTO

ARUGULA SALAD WITH APPLES, WALNUTS
AND GORGONZOLA CHEESE

GREEN SALAD WITH PEARS, PINE NUTS AND GOAT CHEESE

HARICOTS VERT AND RED POTATO SALAD

ROASTED POTATO SALAD

HERBED TOMATO BREAD SALAD

CONFETTI SALSA

# GRILLED ASPARAGUS

*1 bunch asparagus*
*Extra-virgin olive oil*
*Salt and pepper to taste*

Snap off the woody ends of the asparagus and arrange the spears in a baking dish. Drizzle liberally with olive oil and season generously with salt and pepper.

Arrange the asparagus on a grill rack. Grill until slightly blackened on all sides, turning frequently with tongs. Serve hot, chilled or at room temperature.

*Serves 4*

*THIS RECIPE IS THE EPITOME OF SIMPLICITY AND REALLY MAKES THE NUTTY, EARTHY TASTE OF THE ASPARAGUS SHINE. ALSO, IT TAKES VIRTUALLY NO PREPARATION AT ALL! DON'T FORGET TO PLACE THE ASPARAGUS PERPENDICULAR TO THE GRILL GRATE, SO THEY DO NOT FALL THROUGH.*

# Carrot Soufflé

*1 pound baby carrots*
*1 cup milk*
*3 eggs*
*½ cup (1 stick) unsalted butter, melted*
*¼ cup sugar*
*2 tablespoons all-purpose flour*
*1 tablespoon baking powder*
*¼ teaspoon cinnamon*

Boil the carrots in enough water to cover in a large saucepan until tender; drain. Mash the carrots in a bowl using a hand immersion blender or potato masher. Add the milk and mix until combined.

Whisk the eggs in a bowl until blended. Add the butter, sugar, flour, baking powder and cinnamon and whisk until smooth. Blend the egg mixture into the carrot mixture. Pour into a buttered soufflé dish and bake at 350 degrees for 50 minutes. Serve immediately.

*Serves 4 to 6*

*I WAS ON A PHOTO SHOOT FOR WORK, AND A FRIEND WAS RAVING ABOUT THIS DISH. SHE WAS SINGLE AT THE TIME AND USED TO MAKE IT FOR HERSELF AND EAT THE ENTIRE THING! IT IS SO HEAVENLY THAT I PASS IT OFF AS DESSERT FOR MY THREE BOYS!*

# MAMAGIRL'S CORN PUDDING

*1 (15-ounce) can cream-style corn*
*1 (12-ounce) can evaporated milk*
*3 eggs, beaten*
*¼ cup sugar*
*3 tablespoons cornstarch*
*3 tablespoons unsalted butter, cut into pieces*

Combine the corn, evaporated milk, eggs, sugar and cornstarch in a bowl and mix well. Pour into a buttered baking dish and dot with 3 tablespoons butter. Bake at 350 degrees for 1½ hours or until set. Serve immediately.

*Serves 6 to 8*

*WHENEVER I SPEND A THANKSGIVING DINNER AWAY FROM MY MOM'S KITCHEN, I ALWAYS MISS THIS COMFORTING AND TREASURED DISH. WHEN I MAKE THIS AT HOME, MY OWN KIDS SAY, "MAMAGIRL, MORE CORN PUDDING, PLEASE!"*

# PEAS WITH PROSCIUTTO

*2 tablespoons unsalted butter*
*1 large bunch or 2 small bunches scallions, sliced*
*1 (16-ounce) package frozen petite peas, thawed*
*4 ounces prosciutto, chopped*
*Kosher salt and freshly ground pepper to taste*

Melt the butter in a large skillet and add the scallions. Sauté until the scallions are wilted but not brown. Stir in the peas and prosciutto and sauté until heated through. Season with salt and pepper and serve.

*Serves 4 to 6*

AFTER TOO MANY YEARS OF CANNED PEAS WITH MUSHROOMS AT OUT THANKSGIVING DINNER, MY MOM CAME UP WITH THIS FRESH ALTERNATIVE. BOY, WERE WE ALL THANKFUL!

# GRATIN POTATOES WITH LEEKS AND PORCINI MUSHROOMS

*⅓ cup dried porcini mushrooms*

*1 cup chicken broth, heated*

*2 small leeks, trimmed and sliced (white and light green parts)*

*1 tablespoon olive oil*

*¼ cup (½ stick) unsalted butter, melted*

*1½ cups (6 ounces) grated fontina cheese or Gruyère cheese*

*3 pounds Yukon Gold potatoes, peeled and cut into ¼-inch slices*

*Salt and pepper to taste*

*2 garlic cloves, minced*

Reconstitute the mushrooms in the broth in a bowl for about 20 minutes. Drain the mushrooms through a fine sieve, reserving 2 tablespoons of the liquid. Sauté the leeks in the olive oil in a skillet over medium heat until light brown.

Reserve 1 tablespoon of the butter and ⅓ cup of the cheese for topping. Layer the potatoes, remaining butter, salt, pepper, remaining cheese, garlic, leeks and mushrooms in a buttered 2-quart baking dish until all of the ingredients are used, ending with the potatoes. Drizzle with 1 to 2 tablespoons of the reserved mushroom liquid and the reserved 1 tablespoon butter. Sprinkle with the reserved ⅓ cup cheese.

Bake, covered with foil, at 350 degrees for 30 minutes. Remove the foil and bake for 30 to 40 minutes longer or until the top is brown and crusty. If the potatoes are tender, but the top is not golden brown, you may broil for several minutes.

*Serves 8*

*THESE ARE AN ABSOLUTE FAMILY FAVORITE, ONE THAT I AM FREQUENTLY ASKED TO BRING TO FESTIVE GATHERINGS. THERE ARE NEVER ANY LEFTOVERS, AND GUESTS ARE SURE TO SNEAK BACK TO THE BUFFET FOR SECOND AND THIRD HELPINGS!*

# Twice-Baked Potatoes

*6 Idaho baking potatoes, baked*
*2 cups (8 ounces) shredded Cheddar cheese*
*½ cup sour cream*
*½ cup milk*
*1 bunch scallions, chopped (white and some green parts)*
*1 tablespoon parsley, chopped*
*2 tablespoons unsalted butter, melted*
*1 teaspoon salt*
*Melted butter for brushing*

Cut the hot potatoes lengthwise into halves and scoop the pulp into a bowl, reserving the shells. Arrange the shells in a single layer on a baking sheet.

Mash the pulp until smooth. Add the cheese, sour cream, milk, scallions, parsley, 2 tablespoons butter and the salt and mix until combined. Mound the potato mixture evenly in the shells and brush with melted butter. Bake at 375 degrees for 25 to 30 minutes or until golden brown.

*Serves 6 to 12*

*IF YOU ARE LOOKING FOR A HEARTY SIDE DISH THAT YOU CAN PREPARE AHEAD OF TIME FOR AN EVENT, YOU'VE FOUND IT. I MADE THESE TWICE-BAKED POTATOES FOR MY FIRST DINNER PARTY. THEY ARE AN EASY AND DELICIOUS CROWD PLEASER!*

# SAUTÉED SPINACH WITH GARLIC AND GOLDEN RAISINS

*¾ cup orange juice*
*½ cup golden raisins*
*3 tablespoons olive oil*
*3 garlic cloves, minced*
*2 pounds fresh baby spinach leaves*
*Kosher salt and freshly ground pepper to taste*
*¼ cup pine nuts, toasted*

Combine the orange juice and raisins in a microwave-safe bowl. Microwave on High for 30 seconds or until warm. Let stand until needed. The raisins will plump and sweeten in the orange juice.

Heat the olive oil in a large sauté pan over medium heat and add the garlic. Sauté for 1 minute; do not allow the garlic to burn. Drain the raisins and add to the sauté pan. Stir in the spinach, salt and pepper.

Cook for 3 minutes or until the spinach wilts, stirring constantly. Remove from the heat and spoon into a serving bowl. Sprinkle with the pine nuts. Serve immediately.

*Serves 4*

*TWELVE YEARS AGO, WHEN I WAS A NEWLYWED AND IT STILL FELT LIKE MY HUSBAND AND I WERE PLAYING HOUSE, I COOKED MY WAY THROUGH THE NEW BASICS AND MARTHA STEWART LIVING AND LEARNED TO COOK BY TRIAL AND ERROR. THIS WAS ONE OF MY FIRST GOOD RECIPES THAT I HAVE RETURNED TO TIME AND AGAIN.*

# Maple Sweet Potatoes

*2 pounds sweet potatoes, peeled, or*
    *1 (36-ounce) can sweet potatoes*
*½ cup (1 stick) unsalted butter*
*¼ cup pure maple syrup*
*¼ cup packed brown sugar*
*¼ teaspoon cinnamon*
*⅛ teaspoon nutmeg*
*Grated zest of 1 orange (optional)*
*Salt to taste*

Boil the fresh sweet potatoes in enough water to cover in a saucepan until tender-crisp. Drain and cut into quarters. Bring the butter, syrup, brown sugar, cinnamon and nutmeg to a boil in a saucepan, stirring occasionally. Remove from the heat and stir in the orange zest.

Arrange the sweet potatoes in a buttered 2-quart ceramic baking dish and pour the syrup evenly over the top. Season with salt. Bake at 350 degrees for 35 to 40 minutes or until light brown around the edges.

*Serves 8*

*THESE HAVE BEEN A STAPLE AT OUR THANKSGIVING TABLE FOR OVER TWENTY-FIVE YEARS. I ONCE TRIED TO ELIMINATE THEM FROM THE MENU, BUT WAS FORCED TO MAKE THEM AT THE LAST MINUTE BY MY BROTHER, WHO JUST COULD NOT ENJOY HIS DINNER WITHOUT THEM.*

# Zucchini Genovese

*1 cup (about) vegetable oil*
*6 small to medium zucchini, cut into ¼-inch slices*
*Salt and freshly ground pepper to taste*
*1 garlic clove, cut into 3 or 4 slices*
*3 to 4 tablespoons red wine vinegar*
*¼ cup fresh mint leaves*

Add enough of the oil to a deep skillet to measure ¼ inch and heat until hot. Fry the zucchini slices in the oil for 2 to 3 minutes per side or until golden brown. Remove the slices to a shallow dish using a slotted spoon. Season with salt and pepper and sprinkle with the garlic. Drizzle with the desired amount of vinegar and mix in the mint leaves.

*Serves 4 to 6*

THE FIRST TIME I HAD THIS DISH I WAS IN THE NORTHERN PART OF ITALY. IT IS A STAPLE OF ANTIPASTI PLATTERS. YOU CAN MAKE IT AHEAD AND SERVE IT AT ROOM TEMPERATURE OR EVEN COLD. THE ACID IN THE VINEGAR MIXES WITH THE OIL TO FORM A DO-IT-YOURSELF VINAIGRETTE.

# QUICK RISOTTO

*1 tablespoon olive oil*
*1 tablespoon unsalted butter*
*1 cup chopped Spanish onion*
*2 cups beef broth*
*1 cup long grain rice*
*¼ cup (1 ounce) grated Parmesan cheese*

Heat the olive oil and butter in a saucepan until the butter melts. Add the onion and sauté until tender. Add the broth and rice and bring to a boil. Reduce the heat.

Simmer, covered, for 20 minutes. Remove from the heat and fluff the rice with a fork. Spoon into a serving bowl and sprinkle with the cheese. Serve immediately.

*Serves 4*

*My great-grandmother had five children and was a fantastic cook. She would call this rice dish a "quick" version of risotto. It is a satisfying weekday side dish with roasted chicken, and whenever I make it for company they rave!*

# CITRUS, RADICCHIO AND ENDIVE SALAD

**SHERRY CITRUS DRESSING**

½ cup sherry vinegar

6 tablespoons walnut oil or light olive oil

¼ cup canola oil

1 tablespoon honey

½ teaspoon salt

**SALAD**

2 pink grapefruit, supremed

2 white grapefruit, supremed

2 navel oranges, supremed

2 blood oranges, supremed

1 head radicchio, torn into bite-size pieces

2 heads Belgian endive, cut into
   bite-size pieces

4 cups field greens

½ cup chopped red onion

To prepare the dressing, whisk the vinegar, walnut oil, canola oil, honey and salt in a bowl until blended.

To prepare the salad, peel the fruit with a sharp knife, completely removing the pith. Supreme the fruit by cutting carefully between the membranes. Carefully separate the sections. Mix the radicchio, endive and field greens in a salad bowl. Add half the dressing and toss to coat. Arrange the grapefruit sections and orange sections over the salad greens and sprinkle with the onion. Drizzle with the remaining dressing.

*Serves 10 to 12*

THIS IS A WONDERFUL SALAD WHICH I OFTEN SERVE AT BRUNCH. EVERYONE WHO HAS TRIED IT HAS ASKED FOR THE RECIPE. THE COMBINATION OF FRUIT AND BITTER GREENS WITH THE SLIGHTLY SWEET DRESSING MAKES FOR A PERFECTLY BALANCED AND REFRESHING SALAD.

# CRUNCHY COCONUT AND WATERCRESS SALAD

### SALAD

1 coconut

1 bunch scallions

2 red bell peppers, julienned

1½ ripe mangoes, julienned

5 bunches watercress, trimmed and chopped

1 cup frozen peas, thawed

### SPICY LIME VINAIGRETTE

1 teaspoon grated fresh ginger

1 jalapeño chile, seeded and finely minced

Grated zest and juice of 3 limes

7 tablespoons good-quality olive oil

Salt and pepper to taste

To prepare the salad, crack and peel the outer shell of the coconut. Grate the flesh. (You can purchase fresh coconuts in the produce section of many supermarkets that have been cracked, shelled and shrink-wrapped.) Chop the scallion bulbs and some of the green tops. Toss the coconut, scallions, bell peppers, mangoes, watercress and peas in a bowl.

To prepare the vinaigrette, mix the ginger, chile and lime zest in a bowl. Stir in the lime juice and then whisk in the olive oil until the oil is emulsified. Season with salt and pepper. Toss the salad with the vinaigrette just before serving.

*Serves 6 to 8*

*THIS CRUNCHY SALAD WILL TAKE YOU AWAY TO A SANDY BEACH IN BALI WITH A RUM PUNCH IN HAND!*

# DEEP-DISH LAYERED SALAD

*1 head iceberg lettuce, shredded*
*¼ cup sliced scallions*
*¼ cup sliced celery*
*1 (6-ounce) can water chestnuts, drained*
*2 (10-ounce) packages frozen peas, thawed*
*2 cups mayonnaise*
*1 tablespoon sugar*
*1 pound bacon, crisp-cooked and crumbled*
*3 eggs, hard-cooked and sliced*
*3 tomatoes, sliced*
*Grated Parmesan cheese to taste*

Layer the lettuce, scallions, celery, water chestnuts and peas in the order listed in a salad bowl. Spread the mayonnaise over the top, sealing to the edge. Sprinkle with the sugar. You may prepare up to this point several hours in advance and store, covered, in the refrigerator.

Just before serving, sprinkle with the bacon and eggs. Layer with the tomatoes and sprinkle with cheese. Serve immediately.

*Serves 6 to 8*

IF YOU HAVE ONE, ARRANGE THIS IN A GLASS BOWL; THE DIFFERENT COLORED LAYERS MAKES FOR A BEAUTIFUL PRESENTATION. WHENEVER MY MOM MADE THIS SALAD, THERE WERE NEVER ANY LEFTOVERS.

# Minted Chicken and Cabbage Salad

**CHILE LIME DRESSING**

1 onion, thinly sliced

2 jalapeño chiles, seeded and chopped

2 garlic cloves, minced

3 tablespoons fresh lime juice

3 tablespoons fish sauce

3 tablespoons canola oil

2 tablespoons sugar

1 tablespoon rice vinegar

Pepper to taste

**SALAD**

¼ cup raw peanuts

4 cups finely shredded cabbage (white, purple or a combination)

2 cups shredded roasted or poached chicken

1 cup shredded carrots

½ cup shredded fresh mint

¼ cup cilantro, cut into shreds

Salt and pepper to taste

To prepare the dressing, combine the onion, chiles, garlic, lime juice, fish sauce, canola oil, sugar and vinegar in a jar with a tight-fitting lid and seal tightly. Shake to combine. Season with pepper. Let stand for 30 minutes or longer to allow the flavors to blend.

To prepare the salad, roast the peanuts in a dry skillet until golden brown. Let stand until cool. Coarsely pound or grind the peanuts until chunky. Toss the cabbage, chicken, carrots, mint and cilantro in a bowl. Add the dressing and toss to combine. Season with salt and pepper. Just before serving, spoon the salad onto a serving platter and sprinkle with the peanuts.

*Serves 4 to 6*

*I HAVE MADE THIS SALAD FOR EVERY BABY SHOWER AND WEDDING SHOWER THAT I HAVE HOSTED OR ATTENDED. IT IS LIGHT, CRUNCHY, REFRESHING, AND ORIGINAL. SHREDDING THE HERBS, NOT CHOPPING, MAKES ALL THE DIFFERENCE.*

# SHRIMP AND WHITE BEAN SALAD

*1 pound large shrimp*
*4 cups rinsed drained cannellini beans (about 3 cans)*
*4 large ripe tomatoes, chopped*
*¼ cup sliced scallions (white and some green parts)*
*2 to 3 tablespoons fresh basil, chopped*
*½ cup olive oil*
*Salt and freshly ground black pepper to taste*
*Red pepper flakes to taste*

Bring a stockpot three-fourths full of water to a boil and add the shrimp. Return to a boil and boil for 3 to 4 minutes or until the shrimp turn pink. Drain, reserving the cooking liquid. Let the cooking liquid stand until cool. Peel and devein the shrimp.

Place the beans and tomatoes in a colander. Pour the reserved cooking liquid over the bean mixture and drain. Combine the shrimp, beans, tomatoes, scallions and basil in a bowl and mix gently. Add the olive oil and mix to coat. Season with salt, black pepper and red pepper flakes. Serve at room temperature or chilled.

*Serves 8*

*THIS IS A GREAT DISH FOR A BABY SHOWER, BRIDAL SHOWER, OR LADIES LUNCHEON. I FIRST HAD IT AT MY OWN WEDDING SHOWER.*

# SEAFOOD PASTA WITH LEMON SAFFRON HERB DRESSING

### PASTA

16 ounces fusilli or similar shape pasta

Salt to taste

1 tablespoon lemon juice

1 tablespoon extra-virgin olive oil

### SAFFRON HERB DRESSING AND ASSEMBLY

1/8 teaspoon crushed saffron threads

1/2 cup light mayonnaise

1/2 cup sour cream

6 tablespoons lemon juice

5 tablespoons extra-virgin olive oil

1/2 cup thinly sliced scallions (white and some green parts)

2 tablespoons minced fresh tarragon

2 tablespoons drained capers

1 tablespoon minced fresh dill weed

1 teaspoon sugar

Salt and pepper to taste

1 pound deveined peeled cooked large shrimp, sliced horizontally into halves

1 cup finely chopped celery

8 ounces Dungeness crab meat

Arugula

To prepare the salad, cook the pasta in boiling salted water in a stockpot until al dente, stirring occasionally. Drain, reserving 1/2 cup of the cooking liquid. Place the pasta in a large bowl and drizzle with the lemon juice and olive oil, tossing to coat. Let stand until room temperature, stirring occasionally.

To prepare the dressing, pour 3 tablespoons of the reserved cooking liquid into a medium bowl and sprinkle with the saffron. Let stand at room temperature for 5 minutes. Add the mayonnaise, sour cream, lemon juice, olive oil, scallions, tarragon, capers, dill weed and sugar and whisk until combined. Season with salt and pepper. Pour the dressing over the pasta. Mix in the shrimp and celery, adding the remaining reserved cooking liquid by tablespoonfuls if the mixture is too dry. Fold in the crab meat. Chill, covered, for 1 to 4 hours. Spoon the pasta salad onto a serving platter lined with arugula. Garnish with lemon wedges, sprigs of tarragon and sprigs of dill weed.

*Serves 6 to 8*

THIS PASTA SALAD IS ELEGANT ENOUGH FOR ANY SPECIAL OCCASION. IT IS PERFECT FOR A BRIDAL SHOWER OR ANY CELEBRATION IN THE SPRING OR SUMMER.

# PASTA PRONTO

*½ cup extra-virgin olive oil*
*1 pint grape or cherry tomatoes, cut into halves*
*1 garlic clove, finely chopped*
*Kosher salt and freshly ground pepper to taste*
*1 pound fresh mozzarella cheese, cut into bite-size chunks*
*1 pound cavatappi or rigatoni*
*¼ cup fresh basil leaves, cut into shreds or thin strips*

Combine the olive oil, tomatoes, garlic, salt and pepper in a large bowl and mix gently. (May be prepared up to 6 hours in advance.)

Bring a stockpot of salted water to a boil. Add the cheese to the tomato mixture while the water is coming to a boil. Add the pasta to the boiling water and cook using the package directions. Drain; do not rinse. Add the hot pasta to the tomato mixture and mix well. Stir in the basil and serve immediately.

*Serves 4 to 6*

*My aunt, who lives in Rome, Italy, calls this Pasta Pronto. They make it during the summer, assembling everything but the pasta, while they go to the "sea" all day. When they return from the beach, they boil some water and pronto—dinner! The hot pasta will soften the mozzarella and help meld the flavors together.*

# ARUGULA SALAD WITH APPLES, WALNUTS AND GORGONZOLA

### SHERRY VINAIGRETTE
½ cup olive oil
¼ cup walnut oil
¼ cup sherry vinegar
1 shallot, finely chopped
Salt and pepper to taste

### SALAD
2 or 3 heads Belgian endive, sliced
    horizontally into 1-inch pieces
1 head radicchio, torn into bite-size pieces
4 to 5 cups baby arugula
2 Granny Smith apples, peeled and cut into
    ⅛- to ¼-inch slices
1 cup crumbled Gorgonzola cheese
1 cup walnuts, toasted and coarsely chopped

To prepare the vinaigrette, whisk the olive oil, walnut oil, vinegar and shallot in a bowl until combined or pulse in a blender. Season with salt and pepper.

To prepare the salad, toss the endive, radicchio, arugula, apples and vinaigrette in a bowl to coat. Sprinkle with the cheese and walnuts and toss. Serve immediately.

*Serves 8*

*I MAKE THIS SALAD QUITE OFTEN, ESPECIALLY WHEN THE MENU CAN HANDLE A HEARTIER FIRST COURSE. IT HAS THE PERFECT BALANCE OF SALT, SWEET, AND CRUNCH.*

# Green Salad with Pears, Pine Nuts and Goat Cheese

**SHERRY VINAIGRETTE**
½ cup olive oil
¼ cup walnut oil
¼ cup sherry vinegar
1 shallot, finely chopped
Salt and pepper to taste

**SALAD**
1 cup pine nuts
2 heads Belgian endive, sliced horizontally
    into 1-inch pieces
1 head radicchio, torn into bite-size pieces
4 cups spring salad mix
2 cups baby arugula
4 Bosc pears, peeled and cut into
    ⅛- to ¼-inch slices
1 cup crumbled goat cheese, feta cheese or
    Montrachet cheese

To prepare the vinaigrette, whisk the olive oil, walnut oil, vinegar and shallot in a bowl until combined or pulse in a blender. Season with salt and pepper.

To prepare the salad, toast the pine nuts in a dry skillet until light brown, shaking the pan frequently to ensure the pine nuts do not burn. Toss the endive, radicchio, spring mix, arugula and pears in a bowl. Add the vinaigrette and toss to coat. Sprinkle with the cheese and pine nuts. Serve immediately.

*Serves 6 to 8*

*I DON'T EVEN RECALL HOW THIS RECIPE WAS BORN, BUT IT HAS BEEN IN MY REPERTOIRE FOR YEARS WITH ADAPTATIONS ALONG THE WAY. IT IS ONE OF MY FAVORITE SALADS TO SERVE FOR BRUNCH, OR A SATISFYING ACCOMPANIMENT AT LUNCH OR DINNER.*

# Haricot Vert and Red Potato Salad

*1 pound haricots verts (young tender green beans)*
*3 pounds small red potatoes*
*Salt to taste*
*3 tablespoons dry white wine*
*1 cup good-quality olive oil*
*2 tablespoons Champagne vinegar or white wine vinegar*
*1 large shallot, chopped*
*1 tablespoon coarse Dijon mustard*
*1 large garlic clove, minced*
*1 pint small grape tomatoes, cut into halves*
*2 to 3 tablespoons chopped fresh parsley*
*Pepper to taste*

Cook the beans in boiling water in a saucepan for 3 to 4 minutes or just until tender; drain. Plunge the beans into a bowl of ice water immediately to stop the cooking process. Drain and pat dry with paper towels. Cook the potatoes in boiling salted water in a saucepan until tender; drain. Slice the potatoes into halves. Place in a bowl and drizzle with the wine. Let stand until cool.

Combine the olive oil, vinegar, shallot, Dijon mustard and garlic in a blender and process briefly. Combine the beans, potatoes, tomatoes, olive oil mixture and parsley in a bowl and toss gently. Season with salt and pepper.

*Serves 12*

*A PERFECT SAVORY SIDE DISH FOR MANY MEAT AND POULTRY ENTRÉES THAT HAS GREAT FLAVOR, TEXTURE, AND COLOR.*

# ROASTED POTATO SALAD

3 pounds small red potatoes, cut into halves
¼ cup olive oil
1 teaspoon dried thyme
1 teaspoon dried rosemary
Kosher salt and freshly ground pepper
   to taste
3 tablespoons rice wine vinegar
1½ tablespoons mayonnaise

1½ teaspoons anchovy paste (optional)
1 small garlic clove, minced
Pinch of salt
2 grinds of fresh pepper
6 tablespoons extra-virgin olive oil
1 large shallot, cut into slivers
1 cup coarsely chopped kalamata olives
¼ cup chopped fresh parsley

Toss the potatoes, ¼ cup olive oil, the thyme and rosemary in a bowl to coat. Season generously with salt and pepper to taste. Arrange the potatoes cut side down on a rimmed baking sheet. Roast at 425 degrees for 25 to 30 minutes or until the potatoes are golden brown; do not stir.

Whisk the vinegar, mayonnaise, anchovy paste, garlic, pinch of salt and 2 grinds of pepper in a bowl until combined. Add 6 tablespoons olive oil by droplets and then in a slow steady stream, whisking constantly until the olive oil is emulsified.

Place the shallot in a large bowl and add the warm potatoes; the shallot will wilt slightly. Add the olives, parsley and mayonnaise mixture and toss to coat. Serve warm or at room temperature. Store the leftovers in the refrigerator.

*Serves 8*

*When you have a big dog and like to travel, you need great dog sitters. I served this salad at a "thank you" dinner for our favorite sitters who are also close family friends. It became an instant classic and works any time of the year.*

# HERBED TOMATO BREAD SALAD

*½ cup extra-virgin olive oil*

*3 tablespoons red wine vinegar*

*2 teaspoons Dijon mustard*

*1 garlic clove, minced*

*1 pound vine-ripened tomatoes, cut into wedges and 1-inch chunks*

*1 pound vine-ripened yellow tomatoes, cut into wedges and 1-inch chunks*

*2½ cups (1-inch) cubes crusty bread*

*½ cup cured pitted black olives*

*¼ cup fresh basil leaves, chopped*

*¼ cup fresh parsley, chopped*

*Salt and pepper to taste*

Whisk the olive oil, vinegar, Dijon mustard and garlic in a bowl until the oil is well blended. Combine the tomatoes, bread, olives, basil, parsley and mustard mixture in a bowl and toss to coat.

Let stand at room temperature for 20 minutes. Season with salt and pepper and serve immediately.

*Serves 4*

*THIS SALAD IS BEST WHEN TOMATOES ARE IN SEASON. FOR A STRIKING PRESENTATION, TRY MIXING DIFFERENT VARIETIES—RED, YELLOW, GREEN, CHERRY, VINE-RIPENED, GRAPE. THIS IS THE QUINTESSENTIAL SUMMER SALAD!*

# Confetti Salsa

*4 ears of corn, shucked and silks removed*
*2 ripe tomatoes, seeded and cut into ¼-inch pieces*
*1 (15-ounce) can black beans, drained*
*1 ripe avocado, cut into ¼-inch pieces*
*½ red onion, cut into ¼-inch pieces*
*⅓ cup olive oil*
*Juice of 1 lime*
*Salt and pepper to taste*
*1 cup fresh cilantro, chopped*

Cook the corn in boiling water in a saucepan for 8 minutes; drain. Let stand until cool and then cut the kernels off the cob into a bowl. Stir in the tomatoes, beans, avocado and onion.

Whisk the olive oil and lime juice in a bowl until blended and season with salt and pepper. Add the dressing and cilantro to the corn mixture and toss to coat.

*Serves 4 to 6*

*THIS IS MY "SEPTEMBER SALAD," WHEN TOMATOES AND CORN ARE AT THEIR BEST. BE CREATIVE AND ADD YOUR FAVORITE EXTRAS. SOMETIMES I ADD WATERMELON; I LOVE THE ADDITION OF DICED WATERMELON, WHICH ADDS TO THE REFRESHING QUALITY OF THIS FUN SALAD.*

# Mount Vernon, New York

*"Gramatan Goodies"*

*Gramatan Avenue, named after Gramatan, Chief of the Mohicans, runs from
Pondfield Road in Bronxville far into the City of Mount Vernon. It is a bustling street with
restaurants and many historic homes.*

Just north of New York City's Bronx border and south of the Town of Eastchester, Mount
Vernon is the eighth-largest city in New York State. With an enormously diverse population
for its size of only 4.4 square miles, Mount Vernon was incorporated in 1853, first as a
village of Eastchester and then separately as a city in 1892. The city's eastern and western
borders are the Hutchinson River and the Bronx River, respectively.

Named after George Washington's estate in Virginia, Mount Vernon is a city rich in
tradition and history. Created with high hopes and modest expectations by a group of like-
minded, hardworking people, Mount Vernon was the first community in Westchester to
be deliberately planned as a suburb of New York City. The 1,107 members of the "Industrial
Home Association No. 1" purchased five farms with a combined area of about 370 acres,
costing approximately $205 per acre, thus beginning the village of Mount Vernon.

The Junior League of Bronxville has forged many successful partnerships with a diverse
group of organizations in Mount Vernon. Some past programs have included the Homeless
Outreach Project and Education program (HOPE) and the Vernon Family Center homeless
shelter, where various services were provided for single parents. Presently, The JLB sponsors
activities for senior citizens at the Wartburg Adult Care Community, a preliteracy program
for preschool-aged children at Mount Vernon Head Start, and Backpack Buddies, a food
assistance program for underprivileged school-aged children.

# GRAMATAN GOODIES
## DESSERTS

BALSAMIC STRAWBERRIES

CHOCOLATE MOUSSE

APPLE CRISP

BLUEBERRY KUCHEN

CINNAMON ICE CREAM SANDWICHES

APPLESAUCE SPICE CAKE

SHOW-STOPPER CHOCOLATE LAYER CAKE

LEMON POPPY SEED CAKE

CHOCOLATE TRUFFLES

PISTACHIO, CHERRY AND WHITE CHOCOLATE BISCOTTI

LIMONCELLO CHEESECAKE BITES

GRANDMA'S DREAM CAKES

OATMEAL CARMELITAS

CASHEW BUTTER COOKIES

KEY LIME CHEESECAKE PIE

# BALSAMIC STRAWBERRIES

*2 pints ripe strawberries*
*¼ cup balsamic vinegar*
*¼ cup sugar*
*Ground pepper to taste*

Cut the strawberries into quarters and place in a bowl. Add the vinegar and sugar and toss gently. Season with pepper. Let the strawberry mixture macerate at room temperature for several hours. Spoon into dessert bowls.

*Serves 6 to 8*

*THE BALSAMIC VINEGAR AND BLACK PEPPER ARE AN UNEXPECTED ADDITION TO THIS EASY FRUIT DESSERT. I LOVE TO SERVE THESE MACERATED BERRIES OVER STORE-BOUGHT ANGEL FOOD CAKE IN THE SUMMERTIME FOR A REALLY EASY, HEALTHY, AND SEASONAL DESSERT. IT'S A GREAT WAY TO END A BARBECUED MEAL!*

# CHOCOLATE MOUSSE

*6 ounces semisweet chocolate*
*½ cup (1 stick) unsalted butter*
*3 egg yolks, lightly beaten*
*3 egg whites*
*2 tablespoons sugar*
*1 cup heavy whipping cream*
*1 teaspoon vanilla extract*

Heat the chocolate and butter in a double boiler over simmering water until blended, stirring occasionally. Pour into a bowl and let stand until room temperature. Stir in the egg yolks.

Beat the egg whites in a mixing bowl until soft peaks form. Add the sugar gradually, beating constantly until stiff peaks form. Whisk a small amount of the egg whites into the chocolate mixture to lighten it and then fold in the remaining egg whites.

Beat the cream and vanilla in a mixing bowl until stiff peaks form. Fold into the chocolate mixture until combined. Spoon the mousse into parfait dishes and chill in the refrigerator. Garnish with sweetened whipped cream before serving.

If you are concerned about using raw eggs, use eggs pasteurized in their shells, which are sold at some specialty food stores, or use an equivalent amount of pasteurized egg substitute.

*Serves 8*

*THIS IS MY NEVER-FAIL RECIPE FOR DINNER PARTIES. REFINED AND ALWAYS PLEASING TO THE PALATE, IT CAN EVEN BE MADE THE DAY BEFORE. TO DRESS IT UP, I LIKE TO PLACE INDIVIDUAL SERVINGS IN ANTIQUE LUSTERWARE TEACUPS, PRETTY SERVING CUPS, OR DELICATE GLASSWARE.*

# APPLE CRISP

*⅔ cup all-purpose flour*
*⅔ cup packed brown sugar*
*1 teaspoon cinnamon*
*¼ teaspoon salt*
*6 tablespoons unsalted butter, cut into small pieces*
*9 McIntosh apples, peeled and thinly sliced (about 3 pounds)*

Mix the flour, brown sugar, cinnamon and salt in a bowl. Cut in the butter using a pastry blender or fork until the mixture resembles coarse meal.

Arrange the apples in a buttered 10-inch baking dish and sprinkle with the brown sugar mixture. Bake at 400 degrees for 25 minutes or until the apples are tender and the topping is golden brown. Serve warm with caramel topping, vanilla ice cream and/or cinnamon ice cream.

*Serves 6 to 8*

*My mom has been making an excellent apple pie since she was twelve years old. One year I brought this apple crisp to our annual Thanksgiving dinner. Only one person had pie that year! Now, it's not Thanksgiving without my apple crisp.*

# BLUEBERRY KUCHEN

*1 cup all-purpose flour*
*2 tablespoons sugar*
*Dash of salt*
*½ cup (1 stick) unsalted butter, cut into small pieces*
*1 tablespoon white vinegar*
*1 cup sugar*
*Dash of cinnamon*
*3 cups fresh blueberries*

Mix the flour, 2 tablespoons sugar and the salt in a bowl. Cut in the butter with a pastry blender until crumbly. Add the vinegar and mix until the mixture forms a ball. Press the dough over the bottom of a 9-inch baking pan. For a fancier presentation, press over the bottom and 1 inch up the side of an 8-inch tart pan.

Combine 1 cup sugar and the cinnamon in a bowl and mix well. Fold in 2 cups of the blueberries. Spoon the blueberry mixture over the prepared layer and spread evenly to the side of the pan. Bake at 400 degrees for 1 hour. (If using a dark metal pan, reduce the oven temperature to 375 degrees.) Remove from the oven and sprinkle immediately with the remaining 1 cup blueberries.

*Serves 8*

MY MOM WOULD ALWAYS MAKE THIS QUICK-AND-EASY DESSERT AFTER A DAY OF FAMILY BLUEBERRY PICKING IN MAINE. I HAVE BEGUN MAKING IT NOW AND MY FRIENDS AND FAMILY CAN NEVER GET ENOUGH OF IT.

# CINNAMON ICE CREAM SANDWICHES

*1 pint vanilla ice cream, softened*

*2 tablespoons cinnamon*

*⅔ cup all-purpose flour*

*2 teaspoons cinnamon*

*½ teaspoon baking soda*

*¾ cup (1½ sticks) unsalted butter, softened*

*¾ cup granulated sugar*

*¾ cup packed light brown sugar*

*1 egg*

*2 tablespoons water*

*2 teaspoons vanilla extract*

*3 cups quick-cooking oats*

*1 cup raisins*

Combine the ice cream and 2 tablespoons cinnamon in a bowl and mix well. Repack the ice cream in the ice cream package and freeze.

Sift the flour, 2 teaspoons cinnamon and the baking soda together. Beat the butter, granulated sugar and brown sugar in a bowl until creamy. Add the egg, water and vanilla and mix well. Blend in the flour mixture. Stir in the oats and raisins.

Drop the dough by heaping tablespoonfuls 2 inches apart onto an ungreased nonstick cookie sheet. Bake at 350 degrees for 15 minutes or until the edges of the cookies are brown. Cool on the cookie sheet for 2 minutes. Remove to a wire rack to cool completely.

Allow the ice cream to soften while the cookies are cooling. Sandwich a heaping tablespoon of the ice cream between two cookies and press gently. Wrap the ice cream sandwiches individually in waxed paper and freeze for several hours or until firm.

*Makes 12 to 16*

*Spicy and creamy, these ice cream sandwiches are for grown-up kids—although real kids love them, too! They are easy to make ahead of time for an informal party and keep for ages in the freezer.*

# APPLESAUCE SPICE CAKE

2 cups all-purpose flour

2 teaspoons baking soda

⅛ teaspoon kosher salt

½ cup (1 stick) unsalted butter

1⅔ cups chunky applesauce

1 cup granulated sugar

2 eggs, lightly beaten

2½ teaspoons cinnamon

1 teaspoon ground ginger

1 teaspoon vanilla extract

Pinch of nutmeg

1 cup golden raisins

2 tablespoons confectioners' sugar

2 pints vanilla ice cream

Mix the flour, baking soda and salt together. Melt the butter in a saucepan over medium heat. Remove from the heat and stir in the applesauce, granulated sugar, eggs, cinnamon, ginger, vanilla and nutmeg. Blend in the flour mixture and stir in the raisins.

Pour the batter into a buttered and floured 9-inch springform pan or 9-inch cake pan. Bake at 350 degrees for 35 to 40 minutes or until a wooden pick inserted in the center comes out clean. Cool in the pan on a wire rack for 10 minutes. Loosen the edge of the pan and invert the cake onto the rack. Let stand until cool. Sprinkle with the confectioners' sugar and cut into wedges just before serving. Serve with the ice cream.

*Serves 8 to 12*

*THIS CAKE IS MY QUICK, EASY, GO-TO RECIPE. IT IS THE PERFECT BLEND OF SPICES; WITH THE ADDITION OF THE APPLESAUCE AND NO FROSTING, I'VE EVEN SERVED IT FOR BREAKFAST!*

# SHOW-STOPPER CHOCOLATE LAYER CAKE

**CHOCOLATE LAYER CAKE**
*Unsalted butter for coating*
*All-purpose flour for coating*
*1 cup (2 sticks) unsalted butter, softened*
*3 cups packed light brown sugar*
*4 eggs*
*¾ cup baking cocoa*
*1 tablespoon baking soda*
*2 teaspoons vanilla extract*
*½ teaspoon salt*
*3 cups all-purpose flour, sifted*

*1⅓ cups sour cream*
*1½ cups hot brewed coffee*

**CREAMY CHOCOLATE FROSTING**
*16 ounces cream cheese, softened*
*½ cup (1 stick) unsalted butter, softened*
*8 ounces unsweetened chocolate, melted*
*½ cup brewed coffee, at room temperature*
*4 teaspoons vanilla extract*
*6 cups confectioners' sugar, sifted*

To prepare the cake, coat three 9-inch cakes pans with butter and flour. Cut three circles of waxed paper to fit the pans and press into the pans. Beat 1 cup butter in a mixing bowl until creamy. Add the brown sugar and eggs and beat for 3 minutes or until fluffy. Beat in the baking cocoa, baking soda, vanilla and salt until blended. Add the flour and sour cream one-half at a time, beating constantly until smooth after each addition. Stir in the hot coffee gradually. The batter will be thin. Pour evenly into the prepared cake pans. Bake at 350 degrees for 35 minutes or until the tops are firm to the touch and wooden picks inserted in the centers come out mostly clean, rotating the pans halfway through the baking process. Otherwise, do not open the oven. Cool in the pans for 10 minutes. Remove to a wire rack to cool completely.

To prepare the frosting, beat the cream cheese and butter in a mixing bowl until creamy. Blend in the chocolate. Mix in the coffee and vanilla. Add the confectioners' sugar 1 cup at a time, beating constantly until smooth and fluffy after each addition. Spread between the layers and over the top and side of the cake. Chill, covered, until serving time.

*Serves 8 to 10*

*WHAT COULD BE MORE SHOW-STOPPING THAN A* **THREE**-*LAYER CHOCOLATE CAKE?*

# LEMON POPPY SEED CAKE

**LEMON POPPY SEED CAKE**
3 cups all-purpose flour
¼ cup poppy seeds
1 teaspoon baking soda
½ teaspoon salt
2 cups sugar
1 cup (2 sticks) unsalted butter, softened
4 eggs

Juice of 1 lemon
1 cup plain yogurt
Grated zest of 2 lemons

**LEMON GLAZE**
2 tablespoons unsalted butter
2 cups confectioners' sugar
Grated zest and juice of 1 lemon

To prepare the cake, mix the flour, poppy seeds, baking soda and salt in a bowl. Beat the sugar and butter in a mixing bowl until light and fluffy. Add the eggs one at a time, beating well after each addition. Beat in the lemon juice. Add the flour mixture and yogurt one-third at a time, beating at low speed until combined after each addition. Blend in the lemon zest.

Spoon the batter into a 10-cup fluted cake pan or bundt pan coated with nonstick cooking spray. Bake at 325 degrees for 50 to 65 minutes or until a wooden pick inserted near the center comes out clean. Cool in the pan on a wire rack for 10 minutes. Invert onto the wire rack.

To prepare the glaze, melt the butter in a saucepan over low heat. Add the confectioners' sugar, lemon zest and lemon juice and stir until of a glaze consistency. Drizzle the warm glaze over the warm cake. Let stand until cool.

*Serves 10 to 12*

*AS A KID, THIS WAS ALWAYS ONE OF MY FAVORITE CAKES. IT IS EVEN BETTER SERVED WITH FRESH BERRIES OR YOUR FAVORITE SORBET.*

# CHOCOLATE TRUFFLES

*8 ounces good-quality bittersweet*
*chocolate, finely chopped*
*8 ounces good-quality semisweet*
*chocolate, finely chopped*
*1 cup heavy cream*
*2 tablespoons orange liqueur, hazelnut liqueur,*
*amaretto or any flavor liqueur*
*1 tablespoon brewed coffee*
*½ teaspoon good-quality vanilla extract*
*Baking cocoa and/or confectioners' sugar*

Place the bittersweet chocolate and semisweet chocolate in a heatproof mixing bowl. Heat the cream in a small saucepan just until it comes to a boil. Remove from the heat and let stand for 20 seconds. Pour the hot cream through a fine sieve over the chocolate. Whisk the chocolate mixture gradually until the chocolate is completely melted. Whisk in the liqueur, coffee and vanilla. Let stand at room temperature for 1 hour.

Shape the chocolate mixture by 2 teaspoonfuls into balls and arrange in a single layer on a baking sheet lined with baking parchment; you may also use a melon baller or small ice cream scoop to measure. Coat the truffles with baking cocoa and/or confectioners' sugar. Store, covered, in the refrigerator for several weeks. Serve at room temperature.

*Serves 6 to 8*

*I ALWAYS MAKE THESE FOR MY HUSBAND ON VALENTINE'S DAY. WHAT BETTER WAY TO SAY I LOVE YOU THAN WITH HOMEMADE CHOCOLATES!*

# PISTACHIO, CHERRY AND WHITE CHOCOLATE BISCOTTI

*3 cups all-purpose flour*
*2 teaspoons baking powder*
*½ teaspoon salt*
*1 cup sugar*
*3 eggs*
*2 tablespoons canola oil*
*2½ teaspoons almond extract*

*1 cup dried cherries*
*¾ cup unsalted pistachios*
*½ cup chopped white chocolate*
*8 ounces bittersweet or dark chocolate,*
   *chopped*
*8 ounces white chocolate, chopped*

Mix the flour, baking powder and salt together. Beat the sugar, eggs, canola oil and flavoring in a mixing bowl until blended. Add the flour mixture and beat until smooth. Stir in the cherries, pistachios and ½ cup white chocolate.

Divide the dough into two equal portions. Shape each portion into a 3×12-inch log using moistened fingertips. Arrange the logs 3 inches apart on a cookie sheet lined with baking parchment. Bake at 350 degrees for 30 minutes or until light brown and almost firm to the touch. Cool on the cookie sheet for 30 minutes. Reduce the oven temperature to 325 degrees.

Remove the logs to a cutting board. Line the cookie sheet with new baking parchment. Cut each log crosswise into ¼- to ½-inch slices. Stand the slices upright ¼ inch apart on the prepared cookie sheet. Bake for 20 minutes or until light golden brown. Let stand until cool.

Place the bittersweet chocolate and 8 ounces white chocolate in separate microwave-safe bowls. Microwave each chocolate at 20-second intervals until melted. Dip one end of each biscotti slice in either chocolate or drizzle one or both chocolates over each slice. Let stand until set. Store in an airtight container.

*Makes 3 dozen*

WE GET A FIVE-POUND BAG OF SUCCULENT DRIED CHERRIES FROM MICHIGAN EVERY YEAR. THAT WAY I CAN MAKE THESE ALWAYS-SATISFYING AND INVENTIVE BISCOTTI ALL YEAR-ROUND!

# Limoncello Cheesecake Bites

**BISCOTTI CRUST**

*8 ounces vanilla biscotti or almond biscotti*

*6 tablespoons unsalted butter, melted*

*1 tablespoon grated lemon zest*

**LIMONCELLO CHEESECAKE**

*12 ounces whole milk ricotta cheese*

*8 ounces cream cheese, softened*

*8 ounces light cream cheese, softened*

*1¼ cups sugar*

*½ cup limoncello*

*2 tablespoons grated lemon zest*

*2 teaspoons vanilla extract*

*4 eggs*

*1 tablespoon grated lemon zest*

To prepare the crust, spray the bottom of a 9×9-inch baking pan with nonstick cooking spray. Process the biscotti in a food processor until finely ground. Add the butter and lemon zest and process until the crumbs are moistened.

Press the crumb mixture over the bottom of the prepared pan. Bake at 350 degrees for 15 minutes or until golden brown. Cool in the pan on a wire rack. Keep the oven temperature at 350 degrees.

To prepare the cheesecake, process the ricotta cheese in a food processor until smooth. Add the cream cheese and sugar and process until blended. Add the liqueur, 2 tablespoons lemon zest and the vanilla and process until combined. Add the eggs and pulse until blended.

Pour the cream cheese mixture over the baked layer. Arrange the baking pan in a large roasting pan. Add enough hot water to the roasting pan to come halfway up the sides of the baking pan. Bake for 1 hour. Cool in the baking pan on a wire rack for 1 hour. Chill for 8 hours or for up to 2 days. Cut into bite-size pieces. Sprinkle with 1 tablespoon lemon zest just before serving. Store in the refrigerator.

*Serves 6 to 12*

*THESE SQUARES ARE SO AIRY AND REFRESHING. CUTTING THEM INTO SMALL PIECES GIVES YOU AN EXCUSE TO HAVE JUST A BITE OR TWO!*

# GRANDMA'S DREAM CAKES

*2 cups all-purpose flour*
*½ cup packed brown sugar*
*1 teaspoon salt*
*1 cup (2 sticks) unsalted butter, softened*
*1½ cups packed brown sugar*
*1 cup sweetened dried coconut*
*1 cup chopped walnuts or pecans*
*2 eggs, beaten*
*1 tablespoon all-purpose flour*
*1 teaspoon baking powder*
*1 teaspoon vanilla extract*

To prepare the crust, mix the flour, brown sugar and salt in a bowl. Add the butter and mix well. Pat over the bottom of a 9×9-inch baking pan. Bake at 350 degrees for 15 to 20 minutes or until light brown. Maintain the oven temperature.

Combine the brown sugar, coconut, walnuts, eggs, flour, baking powder and vanilla in a bowl and stir until combined. Spread over the baked crust. Bake for 20 to 30 minutes or until light brown. Cool in the pan on a wire rack. Cut into squares. Store in an airtight container.

*Serves 8 to 10*

THIS IS THE FIRST THING THAT I EVER COOKED WITH MY GRANDMOTHER, WHO IS NOW NINETY-THREE. AS A GIFT, SHE HAD THE RECIPE PRINTED ON A MIXING BOWL, AND I THINK OF HER EVERY TIME I USE IT.

# Oatmeal Carmelitas

*¼ cup all-purpose flour*
*1½ cups caramel ice cream topping*
*2 cups all-purpose flour*
*2 cups rolled oats*
*1½ cups packed brown sugar*
*1 teaspoon baking soda*
*½ teaspoon salt*
*1 cup (2 sticks) unsalted butter, melted*
*1 cup (6 ounces) chocolate chips*

Combine ¼ cup flour and the caramel topping in a bowl and mix well. Combine 2 cups flour, the oats, brown sugar, baking soda and salt in a bowl and mix well. Add the butter and stir until crumbly.

Pat two-thirds of the crumb mixture over the bottom of an ungreased 9×13-inch baking pan. Sprinkle with the chocolate chips and drizzle with the caramel mixture. Sprinkle the remaining crumb mixture over the top.

Bake at 350 degrees for 17 to 20 minutes or until light brown. Cool in the pan on a wire rack and then cut into bars. Store in an airtight container.

*Makes 2 dozen*

*MY MOM'S VERY GOOD FRIEND BROUGHT THIS VERY EASY AND VERY DELICIOUS DESSERT TO A FOURTH OF JULY PRE-FIREWORKS COOKOUT. I HAVE BEEN MAKING THEM EVER SINCE.*

# CASHEW BUTTER COOKIES

*1¼ cups all-purpose flour*
*½ teaspoon salt*
*¾ cup cashew butter*
*½ cup (1 stick) unsalted butter, softened*
*½ cup granulated sugar*
*½ cup packed brown sugar*
*1 egg*
*½ teaspoon vanilla extract*
*All-purpose flour for dipping*
*⅓ cup unsalted roasted whole cashews, chopped*

Gently whisk 1¼ cups flour and the salt in a bowl. Combine the cashew butter, butter, granulated sugar and brown sugar in a mixing bowl. Beat with a mixer fitted with a paddle attachment at medium speed for 2 minutes or until light and fluffy, scraping the bowl occasionally. Add the egg and vanilla and mix until combined. Add the flour mixture and beat at low speed just until combined. Shape the dough into a ball and wrap in plastic wrap. Chill for 1 hour or longer.

Scoop 2 tablespoons of the dough and shape into a ball. Place the ball on a cookie sheet lined with baking parchment. Repeat the process with the remaining dough, arranging the balls 3 inches apart. Flatten the balls with a fork dipped in flour, making a crisscross pattern. Sprinkle with the cashews. Bake at 350 degrees for 16 to 18 minutes or until of the desired crispness. Cool on the cookie sheet for 2 minutes. Remove to a wire rack to cool completely. Store in an airtight container.

*Makes 2 dozen*

*THESE COOKIES ARE A SOPHISTICATED TWIST ON TRADITIONAL PEANUT BUTTER COOKIES. THE CASHEWS IMPART A MILD FLAVOR, WHICH IS RICH AND DELICIOUS. MY HUSBAND DOES NOT LIKE PEANUTS, BUT HE ADORES THESE COOKIES.*

# KEY LIME CHEESECAKE PIE

### GRAHAM CRACKER CRUST
1¼ cups graham cracker crumbs
6 tablespoons unsalted butter, melted
1 tablespoon sugar
1 teaspoon cinnamon

### CHEESECAKE FILLING
1 (14-ounce) can sweetened condensed milk
8 ounces cream cheese, softened

½ cup fresh or bottled Key lime juice
1 teaspoon vanilla extract
1 cup heavy whipping cream, chilled
1 tablespoon sugar
1 teaspoon vanilla extract

To prepare the crust, combine the graham cracker crumbs, butter, sugar and cinnamon in a bowl and mix well. Pat into a 9-inch pie plate. Bake at 350 degrees for 10 minutes. Let stand until cool.

To prepare the filling, beat the condensed milk, cream cheese, lime juice and 1 teaspoon vanilla in a mixing bowl until smooth. Spoon into the prepared crust. Chill, covered with plastic wrap, for 8 to 10 hours.

Beat the cream, sugar and 1 teaspoon vanilla in a mixing bowl until soft peaks form. Spread the whipped cream over the top of the pie just before serving.

*Serves 8*

*KEY LIME PIE IS ONE OF MY HUSBAND'S BEST-LOVED DESSERTS. I TRIED AND EXPERIMENTED WITH SEVERAL VARIATIONS UNTIL I CAME ACROSS THIS WINNER. IT IS EFFORTLESS, FOOLPROOF, LIGHT, AND LUSCIOUS. THE CHEESECAKE IS BEST MADE THE DAY BEFORE AND REFRIGERATED OVERNIGHT.*

# MENUS

## Elegant Dinner Party

Endive with Chunky Blue Cheese Dip
Roasted Prime Rib
Gratin Potatoes with Leeks and Porcini Mushrooms
Peas with Prosciutto
Chocolate Mousse
Pomegranate Mojitos

## Sunday Football Fare

Hot Artichoke Dip
Moose's Ribs, Best Ribs Ever!
Chili Stew
Miniature Jalapeño Muffins
Mamagirl's Corn Pudding
Cinnamon Ice Cream Sandwiches
Spicy Bloody Marys

## Autumn Dinner Party

Butternut Squash Apple Soup
Green Salad with Pears, Pine Nuts and Goat Cheese
Chicken, Sausage and Leek Pie
Apple Crisp

# MENUS

### MIDSUMMER NIGHT DINNER

Smoked Trout Mousse
Roasted Potato Salad
Grilled Flank Steak with Rosemary
Grilled Asparagus
Key Lime Cheesecake Pie
Fresh Margaritas

### BRUNCH ON THE PATIO

Banana Mango Bread
Baked French Toast
Homemade Granola
Fresh Fruit with Ginger and Mint
Ruby Red Grapefruit Sparkler

### SPRING DINNER

Figs Filled with Goat Cheese and Prosciutto
Citrus, Radicchio and Endive Salad
Sautéed Scallops and Sweet Pea Risotto
Balsamic Strawberries
Chocolate Truffles

# MENUS

## Do-Ahead Party

MARINATED OLIVES
HUMMUS
CHICKEN MARBELLA
HARICOT VERT AND RED POTATO SALAD
CASHEW BUTTER COOKIES

## Bridal/Baby Shower Brunch

AMERICAN DEVILED EGGS
DEEP-DISH LAYERED SALAD
MINTED CHICKEN AND CABBAGE SALAD
SEAFOOD PASTA WITH LEMON SAFFRON HERB DRESSING
LIMONCELLO CHEESECAKE BITES
WHITE SANGRIA

## Family Birthday Celebration

CHEESEBURGER MEAT LOAF
CARROT SOUFFLÉ
CREAMY MACARONI AND CHEESE
SHOW-STOPPER CHOCOLATE LAYER CAKE

# RESOURCE GUIDE

cherryrepublic.com
All things cherry!

## EASTCHESTER FISH GOURMET
*wonderful selection of fresh fish and seafood*
831 White Plains Road
Scarsdale, New York 10583
914-725-3450, extension 3

## FAIRWAY
*wide variety of fresh produce, cheeses, caviar,*
*extensive meat selection, nuts, oils, vinegars,*
*ethnic foods, dried fruits, breads*
2328 12th Avenue
New York, New York 10027
212-234-3883

## MINI'S PRIME MEATS
*selection of prime meats—special orders accepted*
15 Park Place
Bronxville, New York 10708
914-779-1948

## MRS. GREEN'S
*organic produce, passion fruit purée,*
*nuts in bulk*
780 White Plains Road
Scarsdale, New York 10583
914-472-0111

## TRADER JOE'S
*organic dairy products, nuts, dried fruits,*
*chocolates, smoked fish*
727 White Plains Road
Scarsdale, New York 10583
914-472-2988

## WHOLE FOODS MARKET
*organic produce, fruit juices, organic meats,*
*fish counter, ethnic foods*
100 Bloomingdale Road
White Plains, New York 10605
914-288-1300

## WILLIAMS-SONOMA
*specialty pots and pans, appliances, knives,*
*and baking equipment*
The Westchester Mall
125 Westchester Avenue
White Plains, New York 10601
914-644-8360

MANY OF THESE STORES
HAVE LOCATIONS THROUGHOUT
THE COUNTRY.
LOOK IN YOUR NEIGHBORHOOD
FOR ONE NEAR YOU.

# CONTRIBUTORS

Elizabeth Ackerman

Cathy Alonge

Leslie Anagnostakis

Anne Angevine

Andrea Archibald

Patricia Atkin

Ginger Austi

Kristin Barnard

Lisa Barr

Julie Barry

Andrea Bates

Claudine Bazinet

Virginia Beirne

Priscilla Bender

Elizabeth Brunson

Ellen Bryceland

Julie Cagliostro

Pam Carey

Georgia Ciaputa

Hilary Clark

Jennifer Colao

Carole Crinieri

Tammy Cushman

Kristine Desmarais

Laura Empey

Anne Erblich

Rosanne Fluet

Susan Formato

Raquelle Frenchman

Louise Gabrielle

Allie Galligan

Tracy Gerety

Stephanie Gleason

Shelby Goodrum

Kathy Gray

Nancy Grey

Amy Haggenmiller

Susan Hawkins

Laura Hibbler

Lisa Hofflich

Elizabeth Hole

Dorothy Hong

Kathi Jahnke

Darcy Kaye

Louisa Kinas

Suzanne Klein

# CONTRIBUTORS

Andre Koester

Amy Korb

Jonalie Korengold

Melissa Lamb

Joan Lennon

Joanne Leopold

Jennifer Lupiani

Araxi Macaulay

Candace Martin

Sheryl McCafferty

Marie McKeige

Helena McSherry

Julie Meade

Joann Meehan

Laurie Meehan

Eloise Morgan

Kathryn Mulcahy

Liza Near

Jennifer O'Connor-Parmelee

Sharon Parson

Laura Pettee

Elizabeth Quigley

Christine Rafalko

Susie Reisinger

Beth Risinger

Elisa Shevlin Rizzo

Cathy Rodriquez

Kerry Ryan

Nicole Salimbene

Elizabeth Schaefer

Ginna Sesler

Rita Shea

Nancy Silvestri

Cynthia Shively

Callie St. Phillip

Karen Talbot

Arleen Thomas

Tiffany Tinson

Sandra Tocco

Jennifer Ungvary

Rossana Valentino

Donia Vance

Laura Villani

Nancy Vittorini

Heidi von Maur

Elizabeth Vranka

# INDEX

# INDEX

# INDEX

# INDEX

# INDEX

# Index

# Beyond One Square Mile

## The Junior League of Bronxville

To order, contact
The Junior League of Bronxville, Inc.
135 Midland Avenue
Bronxville, New York 10708

Telephone: 914-793-5097
Fax: 914-793-4206
E-mail: info@jlbronxville.org
Web site: www.jlbronxville.org

# Epilogue

☙❧

In honor of our sixtieth anniversary of service to the community, The Junior League of Bronxville is proud to present *Beyond One Square Mile*, a compilation of favorite recipes from our members and a look at the storied history of the communities we serve.

The Junior League of Bronxville, an organization of women committed to promoting voluntarism, developing the potential of women, and improving the community through the effective action and leadership of trained volunteers, has been involved in community outreach throughout Southern Westchester County, New York, since its founding in the 1940s. While Bronxville is a small suburban village encompassing only one square mile of land, The Junior League of Bronxville actively recruits members from all of the communities it serves, namely, Bronxville, Eastchester, Tuckahoe, Mount Vernon, and Yonkers. Each of these communities has a rich history, diverse population, and varying needs, and it is the mission of the Junior League to identify, and act upon, those many needs.

We, as a League, ventured into the production of this book as both a celebration of our past and a look into our future. Our goal was to bring together all of our members, actives and sustainers alike, to remember and celebrate not only the work we have done, but also the work that is still needed in the many neighborhoods in which we work. Your purchase of *Beyond One Square Mile* will enable our members to continue the tradition of service that was started sixty years ago, continues today, and will flourish for many tomorrows to come. We hope that you will enjoy learning more about the history of The Junior League of Bronxville, as well as the communities we serve, in the following pages. We hope that you will enjoy and share with your families and friends all of the recipes in this book.

On behalf of all our past, current, and future members, all of whom are dedicated to improving the lives of children and families and empowered to provide effective advocacy and direct community service to those in need, thank you for supporting the mission and programs of The Junior League of Bronxville.